European Integration
and American Interests

European Integration and American Interests

What the New Europe Really Means for the United States

Jeffrey Gedmin, Editor

The AEI Press

Publisher for the American Enterprise Institute
WASHINGTON, D.C.
1997

Distributed to the Trade by National Book Network, 15200 NBN Way, Blue Ridge Summit, PA 17214. To order call toll free 1-800-462-6420 or 1-717-794-3800. For all other inquiries please contact the AEI Press, 1150 Seventeenth Street, N.W., Washington, D.C. 20036 or call 1-800-862-5801.

Library of Congress Cataloging-in-Publication Data

European integration and American interests : what the new Europe
  really means for the United States / Jeffrey Gedmin, editor.
        p.   cm.
    ISBN 0-8447-3964-2 (cloth). — ISBN 0-8447-3965-0 (pbk.)
      1. Europe—Economic integration.   2. Europe—Foreign economic
  relations—United States.   3. United States—Foreign economic
  relations—Europe.   I. Gedmin, Jeffrey
  HC241.E8134   1997
  337.4073—dc21   97-10784
                                                             CIP

 1   3   5   7   9   10   8   6   4   2

    ISBN 978-0-8447-3965-6

THE AEI PRESS
Publisher for the American Enterprise Institute
1150 17th Street, N.W., Washington, D.C. 20036

CONTENTS

PART THREE

DEFENSE AND SECURITY

CONTRIBUTORS

STANIMIR A. ALEXANDROV is the former vice minister of foreign affairs of Bulgaria and is foreign counsel with the law firm of Powell, Goldstein, Frazer & Murphy in Washington, D.C. He is also a senior fellow at the International Rule of Law Institute, George Washington University.

CLAUDE E. BARFIELD is a resident scholar and the director of science and technology policy studies at the American Enterprise Institute. His areas of research include international trade, science and technology policy, and U.S. competitiveness.

DENNIS L. BARK, senior fellow of the Hoover Institution, Stanford University, is a political scientist and historian, focusing on Western Europe. He has written and lectured extensively on foreign affairs and relations between Western Europe and the United States, with special emphasis on Berlin and Germany.

CHRISTOPH BERTRAM is the diplomatic correspondent of the German weekly *Die Zeit*. He has published widely on international affairs, in particular on European politics and international security. His most recent publication is *Europe in the Balance: Securing the Peace Won in the Cold War.*

JERMYN BROOKS is the chairman and elected senior partner of Price Waterhouse Europe. He is a frequent lecturer and author on European accounting and governance issues.

WILLARD BUTCHER is a former chief executive officer and chairman of the Board of Directors of the Chase Manhattan Corporation and its principal subsidiary, Chase Manhattan Bank. Since his retirement in 1991, he has been the vice chairman of the International Advisory Committee for the Chase Manhattan Bank, N.A.

BILL CASH is a member of the British Parliament and has been a member of the House of Commons European Select Committee since 1985. From 1989 to 1991, he was chairman of the Conservative Backbench Committee on European Affairs. He is the author of numerous books and pamphlets on Britain and Europe.

PAULA DOBRIANSKY is a senior international affairs and trade adviser at Hunton & Williams in Washington, D.C. She was the director of European and Soviet Affairs at the National Security Council in the Reagan administration.

GERALD FROST is the research director of the New Atlantic Initiative. He has written extensively on political issues in the United States and Britain. He was the director of the Centre for Policy Studies in London and founder-director of the Institute for European Defense and Strategic Studies.

JEFFREY GEDMIN is a research fellow at the American Enterprise Institute, writing and lecturing on German and European politics and U.S.-European relations. He is the author of *The Hidden Hand: Gorbachev and the Collapse of East Germany* and the executive editor and producer of the 1995 PBS documentary, "The Germans: Portrait of a New Nation." In June 1996, he was appointed the executive director of the New Atlantic Initiative.

CHRISTIAN HACKE is a professor of political science at the University of the Armed Forces in Hamburg. His articles on German and American foreign policy appear frequently in *Die Zeit*, *Frankfurter Allgemeine Zeitung*, and *Welt am Sonntag*.

DANIEL HAMILTON is the associate director of the Policy Planning Staff, U.S. Department of State. Before joining the State Department, he had held positions at the Aspen Institute and the Carnegie Endowment for International Peace.

BRIAN HINDLEY is a reader in trade policy in the Department of Economics, London School of Economics, where he has taught since 1967. He is also the cochairman of the Bruges Group.

WERNER HOLZER was the editor in chief of the *Frankfurter Rundschau* from 1973 to 1991. He is the author of several books and has been active as a commentator and moderator for radio and television.

JOSEF JOFFE is editorial page editor and columnist of the *Süddeutsche Zeitung* in Munich and associate of the Olin Institute for Strategic Studies, Harvard University.

HEINZ A. J. KERN is professor of international relations in the Department of International Relations at Boston University.

BURKHARD KOCH is a managing director of Europa Associates Inc., Berlin, and an assistant professor at the Fachhochschule Potsdam. He is the author of *Germany's New Assertiveness in International Relations*.

HANS MARTIN KÖLLE is a financial writer for German and Swiss newspapers. He teaches a course on North Atlantic economic relations at Bonn University. Before returning to Germany in 1989, Mr. Kölle worked for twenty years at the World Bank in Washington, D.C.

MARK P. LAGON is a senior foreign and defense policy analyst for the House Republican Policy Committee, U.S. Congress. He is also an adjunct professor of national security studies, Georgetown University, and associate editor of the journal *Perspectives on Political Science*.

OTTO LAMBSDORFF is the European chairman of the Trilateral Commission. He has been a member of the German Bundestag since 1972. From 1977 to 1984, he was the minister of economics. He is a member of the board of numerous companies.

DAVID MATTHEWS is the editor of the *European Journal*, the journal of the European Foundation.

ALLAN H. MELTZER is a visiting scholar, American Enterprise Institute, and University Professor of Political Economy and Public Policy, Carnegie Mellon University. He was a member of the President's Economic Policy Advisory Board during the Reagan administration and has been an acting member of the President's Council of Economic Advisers and a consultant to the U.S. Treasury and the Board of Governors of the Federal Reserve System.

JOSHUA MURAVCHIK is a resident scholar at the American Enterprise

Institute, an adjunct scholar at the Washington Institute on Near East Policy, and an adjunct professor at the Institute of World Politics. His most recent book is *The Imperative of American Leadership: A Challenge to Neo-Isolationism* (1996).

MANFRED J. M. NEUMANN is the director of the Institute for International Economics, University of Bonn, and the chairman of the Academic Advisory Council to the Federal Ministry of Economics, Bonn.

RICHARD ROSE is the director of the Centre for the Study of Public Policy, University of Strathelyde, Glasgow, and an international scientific adviser, Paul Lazarsfeld Society, Vienna. His latest books are *What Is Europe?* and, with coauthors, *How Russia Votes*.

ERNESTO U. SAVONA is the director of the Research Group on Transnational Crime, School of Law, University of Trento. He is a consultant to the United Nations Crime Programme, Council of Europe, and European Union, as well as a visiting fellow and project director of the National Institute of Justice Research Center, U.S. Department of Justice.

JAMES SHERR is a lecturer in international relations at Lincoln College, Oxford, and a fellow of the Conflict Studies Research Centre, R.M.A. Sandhurst. He is the author of *Soviet Power: The Continuing Challenge*.

RADEK SIKORSKI was Poland's deputy minister of defense in 1992. He is the author of *Dust of the Saints: A Journey to Herat in Time of War*. His book *Full Circle: A Homecoming to Free Poland* will be published in May 1997. He advises Jan Olszewski, the former Polish prime minister.

W. R. SMYSER is the author *The German Economy*.

MICHAEL SPICER has been a member of Parliament in Britain since 1974. His most recent publication is *The Challenge of the East and the Rebirth of the West*.

IRWIN STELZER is the director of Regulatory Policy Studies at the American Enterprise Institute. He is the U.S. economic and political columnist for the *Sunday Times* (London) and the *Courier Mail* (Australia). Mr. Stelzer is the author of *Selected Antitrust Cases: Landmark Decisions* and coauthor of *The Antitrust Laws: A Primer.*

EDWARD STREATOR is the chairman of the New Atlantic Initiative, a member of the executive committee of the International Institute for Strategic Studies, and a director of the South Bank in London. He held positions in the U.S. government as the State Department's director of NATO affairs, deputy permanent representative to NATO, minister at the U.S. embassy in London, and ambassador and permanent representative to the OECD.

MICHAEL STÜRMER is the director of the Research Institute for International Affairs (Stiftung Wissenschaft und Politik), Ebenhausen. He is a columnist for the *Neue Zürcher Zeitung* and the *Financial Times* and an adviser to the EU Commission on Common Foreign Security Policy.

STEPHEN F. SZABO is the associate dean for academic affairs of the Paul H. Nitze School of Advanced International Studies, Johns Hopkins University. From 1982 to 1990, he was associate dean and professor of national security affairs at the National War College, Washington, D.C., and a professorial lecturer in European Studies at SAIS.

NORBERT WALTER is a managing director of Deutsche Bank Research and the chief economist of Deutsche Bank Group.

W. BRUCE WEINROD is a Washington, D.C., attorney and international business and trade adviser. He was the deputy assistant secretary of defense for European and NATO affairs under Secretary of Defense Richard Cheney, director of foreign policy and defense studies at the Heritage Foundation, and a board member of the U.S. Institute of Peace.

JONATHAN WINER is the U.S. deputy assistant secretary of state for law enforcement and crime, Bureau of International Narcotics and Law Enforcement, where he has focused on developing and implementing law enforcement training programs in Eastern Europe and the former Soviet Union. From 1985 to 1993, he was the counsel to U.S. Senator John Kerry.

ACKNOWLEDGMENTS

Many individuals assisted with the organization of this volume. I am indebted to the American Enterprise Institute's president, Christopher DeMuth, and executive vice president, David Gerson, for their interest and generous support. Several interns are to be thanked, especially Alison Gramann and Marieke Widmann. Dana Lane and her editorial staff were extremely helpful. Thanks also to Gwendolyn Wilber, a brilliant young assistant and, for her work on this project in particular, Gwen's equally brilliant colleague, Amanda Schnetzer, a research assistant and program director for the New Atlantic Initiative. Amanda's shepherding of this book was an invaluable contribution.

European Integration and American Interests was the outgrowth of a conference and film that examined numerous new trends in post–cold war Germany and Europe. Important pieces of this work, including this book, were generously supported by the German Information Center in New York, the German Marshall Fund of the United States, and the Smith Richardson Foundation.

INTRODUCTION

Jeffrey Gedmin

With incessant reference to things like the EMU, ECB, IGC, and CFSP, explaining the European Union can be akin to explaining cricket to an American, says one British journalist. At a time when Europeans have been enmeshed in arduous debates cluttered by confusing acronyms, Americans have shown signs of boredom with the Continent. This should come as no surprise. Europeans themselves often appear dismayed and bewildered by the deepening process of European integration, as the quest for monetary and political union is known. In fact, fewer than a third of Europeans can name the current members of the European Union (EU). Fewer claim an even modest grasp of the European Commission or Council of Ministers.

"Almost everybody knows what the Europeans are missing," writes the prestigious German daily, the *Frankfurter Allgemeine Zeitung*. "They say too much that is incomprehensible and decide too little that is important." As for Brussels's bureaucracy, it could drive anyone to distraction. Recent legislation proposed, for instance, that "visually challenged" truck drivers in the EU's fifteen member-states be required to take driving tests without their glasses—after all, glasses could fall off while the driver is at the wheel. But beneath the layers of regulatory zeal and excess lies a continent in the throes of a deep transformation.

In the Dutch city of Maastricht in December 1991, EU governments initialed the Treaty on European Union. By doing so, they charted a course that envisaged a new kind of European Community. Apart from plans for a single European currency, the Maastricht Treaty established two goals: a common justice and internal policy and a common foreign and security policy. If achieved, the monetary and political union of Europe would likely constitute the greatest voluntary transfer of sovereignty in history. It would mean, in the estimation of advocates, a more self-reliant Europe and a stronger partner for the United States. The new union would also create formidable challenges for the United States. As Rudiger Dornbusch writes in the September/October 1996 issue of *Foreign Affairs*, the new Europe, if politically and economically cohesive, could be "financially strong enough to dwarf the United States and the dollar."

1

In fact, the prospects for the kind of union originally envisaged in Maastricht seem remote today. According to the *Economist*, "the present momentum would barely suit a snail." Nevertheless, the Maastricht process has generated a range of serious questions for American policy makers and Europeans alike.

If a single European currency is adopted by the end of the decade, who will the "ins" be, and how will relations develop between those countries included in the monetary union and those excluded? How will this union affect the ambitions of Central European countries to join the EU? Plans for European unity have raised questions about democracy, sovereignty, and the role of the nation-state. How can contradictions be resolved as European governments attempt to transfer important authorities from national capitals to supranational institutions and unelected bodies? What impact will monetary union have on interest rates, unemployment, and the international trading order? What will further steps toward a European security identity mean for stability in Europe and American interests on the Continent?

On these and other questions, the present volume offers a range of commentary, from the Euro-skeptics to the federalists, from the business community to policy makers and leading journalists and academics.

PART ONE
Economy and Trade

INTRODUCTION TO PART ONE

In the changed conditions of the post–cold war world, the relationship between the United States and Europe continues to evolve. Compelling economic and demographic facts are emerging from other regions around the globe. They fascinate and challenge Europeans and Americans alike. New forms of partnership and rivalry have surfaced within the Atlantic community. And, for the Atlantic democracies themselves, a number of recurring questions and themes dominate political discourse. In Europe and in the United States, the welfare state is under assault. Can monetary union in Europe substitute for genuine reform and flexibility in labor markets? Will the creation of monetary and political union make liberalized trade between the United States and the European Union (EU) more or less likely? Could the Euro unseat the dollar as the world's key currency? If a single European currency is adopted by the end of the decade, how will relations develop between the "ins" and the "outs"? What is the likely impact of monetary union on the ambitions of the central European democracies to join the EU?

A Single European Currency and the International Trading System

CLAUDE E. BARFIELD

Resident scholar and director, science and technology policy studies, American Enterprise Institute

A series of recent news and editorial headlines captures the current malaise affecting Europe's economies, and particularly its lead economy, that of Germany: "Chronic Joblessness in Europe," states one; "Europe's Economic Muddle," states another; "Germany Is Not Working," states a third; and "German Unemployment at Highest Level since War," concludes a fourth.

Not all of Europe's current economic woes can be traced to the specific provisions of the Maastricht Treaty. But it must be said that the treaty did little to point Europe in the direction of essential social and economic reforms. In certain respects, most particularly in the Social Charter, the treaty was based on self-deluding assumptions concerning "social dumping" and on the ability of governments to mandate social justice and maintain expensive welfare systems, even though these governments lacked the ability to increase productivity as an offset. In the short term, the drive to put in place a European Monetary Union has forced European Union members to follow Germany's lead and adopt severely deflationary economic policies, which have caused unemployment rates to rise to the highest levels since the 1930s.

Maastricht—EMU

There are two important criteria for governments to meet before they enter the new EMU in 1998: a maximum deficit of 3 percent of gross domestic product and an inflation rate that is not more than 1.5 percent higher than the average of the three countries with the lowest rate of inflation. Given the economic records and practices of most EU countries, these criteria have forced governments to attempt drastic retrenchment over the past several years, with central banks instituting extremely tight monetary policies and politicians attempting, with mixed success, to rein in annual budget outlays.

Efforts to meet the Maastricht budget criteria have also been greatly hampered by events in Germany since 1990. Unification placed a huge burden on the western German economy, and policy misjudgments compounded the German government's difficulties in overcoming obstacles to renewed growth. One such misjudgment was the unilateral decision to raise eastern German wage rates to those of the west immediately, a decision that produced a massive increase in wage costs and the collapse of many eastern German firms. The Bundesbank's tight money policies produced an ever stronger deutsche mark, and the unfavorable exchange rate weakened German export competitiveness, thus cutting off an important source of profit and economic growth.

With other countries' monetary policies tied closely to those of the Bundesbank, when Germany went into recession so did much of the rest of Europe, with particularly strong downward plunges in France, the Benelux countries, and Spain. Only Great Britain and Italy, which opted out of the European currency system, escaped relatively unscathed by the depressing effects of high interest rates.

By mid-1996, the resulting national unemployment rates reached historically high proportions, at least in postwar terms: Belgium, 13.7 percent; France, 11.8 percent; Spain, a staggering 23 percent; and Germany itself, 11 percent. The total number of jobless in the EU currently stands at 18 million.

In the short term, the pressures to comply with EMU conditions will result in continued budgetary stringency. Though both German and French leaders bravely aver that they will meet the EMU criteria by 1998, more realistic projections by the Organization for Economic Cooperation and Development find both falling short of the 3 percent debt of the GDP goal.

Maastricht—The Social Charter

Along with creation of the EMU, the Maastricht decision to grant the central EU governing institutions greater powers over welfare and employment issues through weighted majority voting represented a far-reaching step beyond the original Treaty of Rome's goal of the "free movement of goods, services, capital and people." The Treaty of Rome strongly tilted toward a Europe of "mutual recognition" and competing national systems. Maastricht pointed in the opposite direction toward an EU with substantially top-down decision making, with harmonization and a leveling up of social and employment policies and practices. "Subsidiarity," though much touted

7

as an antidote to centralization, lacked both definition and strong legal standing in the final Maastricht document.

Thus, before a backlash against new central policies appeared in the months after Maastricht, the European Commission stood ready to put into force substantial new rules governing the hours and conditions of employment of both full-time and temporary workers and to pressure governments to match the social safety net provisions of the most developed economies (more paid vacation, paid maternity leaves, and so forth). To buy off the poorer southern, Mediterranean economies, massive subsidies were promised through the "cohesion fund," which aimed to allow these poorer governments to pay for their increased social and employment costs.

The flaws in retrospect were twofold: (1) even if efficiently administered (which it was not), the cohesion fund could not raise Greek or Spanish productivity and thus bid fair to become a subsidy in perpetuity; and (2) since Maastricht, it has become ever clearer that even the rich countries of the north can no longer afford the hugely expensive social welfare systems and the inefficiencies of rigid, protected labor markets.

The EU Social Dilemma

Once again, Germany, the largest economy and historically the central engine of growth for the EU, represents the most illustrative model of the complexities and contradictions that EU governments face as they seek renewed economic vigor.

Athough, admittedly, German reunification and the concomitant discipline of the stringent EMU criteria greatly complicated the task of economic renewal, these factors only exposed more quickly and more starkly the fundamental structural flaws in the German social compact. In 1980, labor costs in Germany and the United States were roughly equal; today, German labor costs are the highest in the world, some 40 percent above those of the United States.

And despite a historic tradition of work discipline, German workers now enjoy the shortest workweek and the shortest working lives of workers in all industrial nations. German workers put in an average of 1,602 hours per year, compared with 1,957 for the Japanese and 1,896 for the Americans. In effect, Americans work an extra seven weeks and Japanese an extra nine weeks compared with their German counterparts.

And Germany is not alone in having daunting employment and

labor problems. Six of the seven industrial countries with the highest manufacturing labor costs are members of the EU. In all these countries, almost 50 percent of total compensation covers areas beyond salary, such as vacation, health, and unemployment benefits.

The excessive costs of adding jobs have forced EU corporations to be extremely cautious in adding to employment. While the United States added some 18 million jobs between 1984 and 1994, the EU added only about 3 to 4 million, most of which were in the public sector. In addition, European unemployment tends to be of much longer duration than U.S. unemployment. A study conducted during the late 1980s found that in the EU about 55 percent of the unemployed had been out of work for more than a year; in the United States only 7 percent were in this category. (The length of unemployment is partially the result of extremely generous unemployment compensation programs, which in some cases give benefits of 80 to 90 percent of former salaries for several years.)

And finally, in the EU, despite former U.S. secretary of labor Robert Reich's claims about the great success of youth and apprentice programs, young people suffer disproportionately from unemployment. In France, 20 percent of young workers are unemployed, and in Spain 40 percent of workers under the age of twenty-five are unemployed.

Belatedly, both Germany and France have committed to significant reforms of both the labor market and the social welfare system. But both the Kohl and the Chirac governments have encountered heavy resistance from powerful interest groups and opposition parties. The Kohl government has announced the boldest plan, including a freeze on public-sector wages, reduction of public spending from 50 to 46 percent of the gross domestic product by the year 2000, reduction of sick pay benefits, and relaxation of job protection for workers in small companies. And Chirac is committed to a similar but less stringent program.

Both face major obstacles: growth in Germany and France is now predicted to be an anemic 1–1.5 percent in 1996, and government revenues in both countries are already falling short of predictions.

Implications for the United States and for the World Trading System

European leaders (particularly Kohl) have thus far strongly and commendably resisted the temptation to turn inward and raise protectionist barriers. But if growth should stall and unemployment should remain at record levels, then even if protectionists' pressures were reined in, there is little likelihood that the EU would agree to further liberalization in the World Trade Organization, even through regional or bilateral arrangements with the United States.

EU agriculture ministers have already vetoed further agricultural liberalization with East European countries; and France, Spain, Greece, and Portugal have expressed reservations about market-opening negotiations with the East Asian and South American countries. The test will come when, sometime in the next several years, the United States once again champions either multilateral or regional liberalization. If, as many trade experts in the United States are predicting, the EU balks, the United States is likely to go it alone and embark on a path that will inevitably lead to an ominous fragmentation of the world trading system. Such an outcome is not foreordained, but it is possible.

Monetary Union: A European Business Perspective

JERMYN BROOKS

Chairman and elected senior partner, Price Waterhouse Europe

Can one start a political essay with personal reminiscences? Let me try. Two key experiences have fashioned my own views on Europe. First, as a schoolboy and later as an undergraduate studying languages and traveling on every occasion possible around Europe, I was struck by the visible signs of the ravages of war in the immediate postwar period of the 1950s and early 1960s. Unifying the Continent politically must surely be a way to overcome the previous hundred years of border conflicts, many of which had led to worldwide conflagration.

Second, in my thirties, as a business partner in Iran (a venture brought to an abrupt end by the revolution), I compared the excitement and enthusiasm of development in a fast-growing economy with the short-term views and petty nationalistic feuds in the tired, old nation-states of Europe. Of course, both views are simplistic, but they serve to remind us that the signatories of the Treaty of Rome were inspired by the will to bury political conflict in Europe and to encircle the nation-states with a benevolent democratic structure that would further political security as well as economic well-being.

Sadly, if we can draw any lessons from history, then certainly our inability to learn from previous generations must be one of them. Apart from the political vision of the current German chancellor and an underlying pro-European Union sentiment in Holland and Italy, the later 1990s demonstrate a return to largely nationalistic thinking in most European countries, ironically, despite the demonstrable and enormous success of the EU on the economic front.

As in business, political change processes are more easily engineered when disaster is approaching or recently overcome. The opportunity for overcoming some of the narrowly focused self-interest of the nation-state was strongest with the vivid memory of the death and destruction wrought by two world wars and the economic misery that followed. This was the period of burying differences and, at least in continental Europe, of looking for a larger ideal that could embrace victor and vanquished alike. As the memory of disaster dims, awareness of the dangers of selfish behavior by individual nations decreases. Sectarian or national interests begin to prevail over regional or international priorities. We increasingly observe those sentiments in Europe in the 1990s, particularly in the views of British Euro-skeptics but certainly not confined to them.

Critical Issues

So despite the economic growth and interdependency achieved by European Union states, what is likely to happen with the Maastricht agreement and at the Intergovernmental Conference to decide the next steps in the EU? The issues are critical: expansion of the EU to Eastern Europe, changes to the institutions and decision-making processes to enable the enlarged union to function politically, and, as an important symbol, the introduction of a single currency. These questions are fundamental as they depend on the vision for Europe of the participating nations and therefore answer the question about the region's direction either toward a Fortress Europe or a more liberal trading environment.

The first question is, What is Europe? If the EU understands itself to be representative of the whole geographic area of Europe, it must hold itself open for any European nation that enjoys democratic structures to join. Normally, Poland, the Czech Republic, and Hungary are thought of in this context, but the number of countries is many times these three with the Baltics, the Balkan countries, and even certain countries of the Commonwealth of Independent States as candidates. If new countries join—and the more who join, the more urgent the issues—the greater the need both to redesign EU institutions and decision-making processes and to find funds to support the much poorer countries' entry into the club.

Finances could be the most critical problem created by enlargement. The need to support agriculture and industry in the new member-states could encourage protectionism, resulting in closing trade access to other than EU members. The liberal trade views of Britain and Germany could possibly be drowned out by the budgetary pressures of integrating new member-states. It will therefore be key not to rush the extension of the EU before the existing fifteen members have decided what type of union they are prepared to support.

Of course, the irony of the situation is that unanimous agreement is required to accept a system of majority voting, which will be essential for real legislative progress. The movement to greater political and economic union is currently proceeding at a snail's pace, the lowest common denominator of what all fifteen members can agree to (or at least thirteen to fourteen of them) with minority views—and exemption from the relevant agreement—expressed by one or two members. The logical way forward would be for those EU states prepared to be bound by majority voting—after all, not a very revolutionary idea—to move toward a closer union, with those unwilling to follow exempted from the agreement or leaving the union altogether.

A Single Currency

Once majority voting is established, supported by greater democratic control of EU institutions through an enhanced role for the European Parliament, the EU can move to greater alignment of economic policies. The coordination of fiscal, budgetary, and monetary policies is a prerequisite for the effective operation of a European central bank and the secure introduction of a single currency. This is, of course, the significance of the convergence criteria of the

Maastricht agreement. And there is no doubt that for the individual citizen of the EU, a single currency would be an even more important everyday reminder of the changed European environment than his right to vote for the European Parliament.

But what would the single currency mean for business? According to estimates, current transaction costs of coping with the many different European currencies total some $20 billion per year. Certainly, the inefficiencies of handling, dealing in, and recording the fifteen different currencies of the fifteen EU states are very great. Even those, mainly the banks, that profit from a multicurrency environment could be the winners from a Euro currency, as it is likely to assume a significance in world trade greater than the deutsche mark and pound sterling combined and to reach trading volumes similar to the yen and U.S. dollar, or even to exceed them.

Even the one-time cost of transforming information technology systems and back offices to deal with the new currency is unlikely to be wasted, provided sufficient advance warning is given by the EU of the phased introduction. IT systems and business processes need regular renewal or update in any case, so that businesses are likely to profit from the obligation to change by introducing improvised cash transaction and recording systems, which together with reduced currency-related costs, will provide competitive advantage.

The main issue therefore surrounding currency union is whether the obvious economic advantages—improved systems, reduced costs, and reduced barriers to exchange of goods and services across European "frontiers"—will be sufficient for European politicians to lead their electorates rather than hide behind opinion poll results. Those polls, of course, show that Europeans prefer their own francs, florins, etc., which they know, to a "Euro," which they do not. The number of currency reforms in many European countries over the past one hundred years indicates that populations very quickly adapt to revised currency units, descriptions, and values—from the *nouveau franc* to the disappearance of 240 pence in the pound!

Conclusion

It is fashionable even in Europhile circles to welcome the (economic) achievements of the EU to date but to decry the need for any further steps toward political integration: there is no need to surrender national sovereignty. A modified version of the same sentiment holds that the benefits of economic alignment, if maintained over a number of years, will in time create the climate for political union. Therefore, the argument goes, we should not attempt to push forward now an integration that is not fully supported by the fifteen EU states.

Perhaps a slower unification could indeed happen. But Europe would do well not to forget the primacy of political decisions over economic activity in all we do. A change in political orientation alters the rules within which business can flourish or lose competitive advantage. A political veto as we saw with de Gaulle or Thatcher was able to set back economic alignment by decades. To compete over the coming decades as an equal with the most successful American and Asian businesses, Europe will need much restructuring and merger activity, probably resulting in three to five major players per industry. To take place efficiently, such major restructuring requires a consistent political will to remove national barriers within Europe and to remain open to international trade. Failing the full opening of borders in Europe and the facilitation of the necessary restructuring, it is more than probable that European countries would fall back into protectionism to save their inefficient national companies from more powerful overseas competitors. An uninterrupted process toward political integration is therefore the only safe platform from which to continue the needed restructuring of business. The global reach of these businesses will drive a spirit of liberalized trade between the EU, the United States, and other countries.

There is just a chance this will happen. But businessmen in Europe need to stand up and be counted. Our politicians need to know that they will have our support if they lead and grasp the opportunities a stronger Europe can provide. Liberal trading arrangements between Europe, the United States, and other major trading nations would be unlikely to survive a failure of the European Union to make its description as both "European" and a "union" closer to reality.

Monetary Union: An American Business Perspective

WILLARD BUTCHER

Former CEO, Chase Manhattan Bank, N.A.

I have been asked to address several questions relative to the European Monetary Union, more specifically how Wall Street views the EMU. Underlying the questions is the premise that not only will the EMU be introduced but both its introduction and its subsequent existence will be highly successful. Before responding to this charge, I am forced at the outset to apologize not once but three times.

First, I am not a foreign exchange professional, and thus my thoughts are from a broad and philosophical perspective rather than a technical one. Second, I apologize for having some real reservations as to whether the EMU will provide stable, accepted European money. This runs counter to the generally held view in Europe, particularly among the government and business elites, that to question the efficacy of monetary union is not only wrong headed but somewhat anti-European. None other than Helmut Schmidt chastised me thoroughly for suggesting mere caution. My third apology is that I need to point out some consequences should the EMU be successfully launched and then unsuccessfully defended.

I am one of the many Americans who have nothing but approbation, appreciation, and applause for the objectives of monetary integration, just as I have been an outspoken advocate for the European Community itself. Those critics of European Union have largely based their arguments on the potential for protectionism. While I am always concerned with protectionism on either side of the Atlantic, I believe that forces beyond the control of Europe or the United States will compel these two powers to stray but little off the path of open, competitive trade and investment. No, my concern is not with the objective but with the belief that a currency can rest neither on gold nor on a body politic graced with the powers of the purse—more specifically, the full range of fiscal and economic levers. Indeed, a currency must rest on something more than the capacity and power of its central bank. How well I remember visiting with Dr. Zijlstra many years ago when he was governor of De Nederlansche

Bank and had just been in The Hague to view the forthcoming national budget. He greeted me with the statement that "no central banker in the world can mop up all of the slop left by his government." Despite promises to the contrary, I predict that things will go awry in one part of Europe or another and that at the same time the European Central Bank will not have sufficient power to arrest it. Do we really believe we can leave the slop-generating powers with fifteen sovereign governments and have on top of it all stable currency?

Economists tell us that there are four ways of dealing with country-specific shocks, that is, adjusting their economies:

- exchange rate adjustment
- labor mobility
- price and wage adjustment
- fiscal transfers

Since there will be no exchange rate to adjust, one must move the labor market flexibility and wage adjustment. Both of these, given the traditions of Europe, are difficult at best. This brings us to fiscal transfers. This issue cannot be addressed without the transfer of considerable political power from the individual governments to the European Union.

Perhaps I am particularly sensitive to this issue because of the early history of the United States. After independence and until the Constitution was adopted in 1787, the central government was a confederation of states, with most of the economic powers left to the states. The national government issued continentals, which became worthless over time. A common expression when I was a boy to describe something of no value was "it isn't worth a continental." While, indeed, some of the decline in value of the continental was due to excessive printing of money to finance the Revolutionary War, in point of fact the government lacked the fiscal and economic powers to stabilize, let alone restore, value after the war. Not until 1792 was monetary reform in the United States possible, as a consequence of the so-called federal powers inherent in the Constitution.

Indeed, the past fifty years are replete with examples of the difficulty of maintaining stable currency values where states possessed the powers but either neglected or misused them. Again, my own country, as well as some European ones, can be cited to support this point.

We have had considerable experience with the exchange rate mechanism. It has worked for Germany and France at some cost to them and has not worked for others to the extent that they were obliged to leave the system. The economies of those that left the system have fared somewhat better and without an outbreak of inflation. In the case of Great Britain, there is some evidence that the pursuit of foreign exchange stability while a part of the system was a cause of subsequent recession.

If a so-called shock occurs after union, a scenario of concern to me would be that, in the absence of adequate fiscal and economic power, the community would find itself with high unemployment. Also a rigid monetary stringency would fall harshly on at least some members of the community whose politicians would be unable to stand the heat and would seek to exit the kitchen with deleterious influence on the stability of the currency. In the extreme, this could be more damaging than solidifying to the cause of European unity.

Some would say that the European Central Bank has been vested with many powers and strictures that go some distance toward the maintenance of currency value. Examples are the "no-bail-out clause," the charge of maintaining price stability, and the prohibition against financing public debt of the member-states. But the bottom-line view is not monetary but fiscal—that is, power over the purse strings—not only taxes but transfer payments. Present transfer arrangements in Europe are not only small but fairly limited to agriculture. Although even the present state of affairs occasionally generates heat within the community, the future requirements for such transfers are of an entirely different magnitude. Neither Maastricht nor other community agreements provide for this critical requirement.

I have heard it is often said and on high authority that political union rests on monetary union. Maybe so. Perhaps, once the egg is scrambled and there is no escape, the transfers of adequate political power will occur. That, however, is a high-risk strategy. I believe that the equation is the other way around; that is, monetary union rests on political union. There is no example in recorded history where a currency separate from a state entity—that is, a political entity—has had permanence. This does not make an anti-union—in fact, quite the opposite—but it does say sound monetary union requires far-reaching *political* change that only Europeans can make.

Fiscal convergence will not be met by any but a few countries by January 1, 1998. I have heard too often calls for loosening the convergence requirements. This will further damage the chances for success. The acceptance of the EMU will be largely determined by its stability, and loosening these requirements will not only reduce stability in and of itself but will signal the willingness of the community to erode discipline further. Even the eventual attainment of fiscal convergence does not suggest its permanence.

But what if the Euro is successfully launched, and the predictions of the Green Book are right; that is, "By the end of the century, the European Union will have a strong and stable single currency"?

What Is the Feeling of Wall Street about the Euro Coming onto the Scene? Unfortunately, one hears far too little about the EMU on Wall Street. In part, this reflects a belief that the EMU will have little effect on the United States; in part, a belief that its introduction will be significantly delayed; and in large part, Wall Street's focus is on the present or near future. Some economists and some corporate planners do follow the developments, especially those with international responsibilities. My unscientific survey suggests that most believe that what we will end up with in the early stages of union will be about what we have now, which probably explains much of the lethargic attitude toward EMU.

Are Americans Looking at EMU as a Potential Threat to U.S. Political Leadership in the Global Arena? The short answer is a loud no. In the post–World War II era, the U.S. dollar has shared reserve currency and quasi-reserve currency status with other currencies, early in these years with the pound sterling and more recently with the deutsche mark and with the yen. Further, the value of the dollar, always a hot topic of conversation, has had its ups and downs—and against the deutsche mark, yen, and Swiss franc mostly downs. The U.S. dollar's relative strength or position in the world has had relatively little impact on the political leadership we provided. That question largely revolved around the correctness of U.S. policy and the willingness of other nations to accept it. Two obvious examples of great import were Vietnam, which most of the rest of the world did not accept, and Desert Storm, which it did. In neither case did the relative strength of the U.S. dollar have any material impact. The relevance, correctness, and acceptance of policy combined with the astuteness and capability of one's policy practitioners will largely determine one's leadership capacity. This will be as true in the future for Europe as for the United States. There is some limit depending on size and economic strength, but both Europe and the United States possess these attributes in sufficient quantity to ensure them a prominent place at the table. What would erode this is massive economic decline, that is, self-imposed economic folly. The vast majority of the business and government elites in the United States have supported over many years a strong and more unified Europe in large part to share the burdens that political leadership implies.

Is the European Union Still a Matter of Concern for Trade-related Issues such as Protectionist Pressure against American Exports?
There are always voices on both sides of the Atlantic advocating protection—in my country, such advocacy finds a voice in both parties. But the potential for calamity is overblown, providing cool heads prevail.

There are always issues between us. Recently, the question of financial services has been the source of some friction, but no one is pressing any hot buttons. The concerns of some ten to fifteen years ago and even during the Uruguay Round have abated to a great extent. In short, there is no paranoia in the United States today about protectionism in Europe. The greatest danger seems to lie in the possibility that monetary union, once imposed, would create those unbearable pressures I previously discussed, which in turn raises a hue and cry for protection. It is, after all, in periods of crisis and decline that protectionism gains currency.

In the meantime, both Europeans and Americans should be vigilant for signs of danger and work tirelessly to resolve issues that stand in the way of mutual trade and investment opportunities. After all, Europe and the United States have a combined gross national product equal to 60 percent of the world and control more than two-thirds of the world's foreign direct investment, having more than $400 billion in each other's economies. I admit to being Eurocentric, but these statistics are powerful arguments for open markets and close friendship.

If All European Countries Join EMU, in 1999 Will the Dollar-Euro Exchange Rate Be Volatile? The theory goes that because of a diversity of European exchange rate movements, an American investor is able to insulate the overall U.S.-European rate from shocks. This, too, is overblown. First, there are many reasons to invest in one country or another, and one will not invest in country A to counterbalance the currency risk in country B. Further, there are many ways to hedge this risk. One is not apt to become an idle investor even if currency movements were triangular—one is always trying to maximize each investment. Finally, which currencies are apt to move in different directions to offset each other? That is a difficult question without a permanent answer.

As a Result of the EMU, Will There Be More of a Two-Way Influence on Interest Rates between Europe and the United States, and Will This Act as a Stabilizing Influence on Economic Growth on Both Sides of the Atlantic? While I am a believer in the theory that if one wants more stable exchange rates, then one's interest rates will be more volatile and vice versa, exchange rates and interest rates are not the only influence on each other. One can have both interest rates and exchange rates highly volatile at the same time as certainly the United States has experienced on occasion in the past two decades. Efforts to decouple the two economies so one feels good on average seem to me highly dubious. It is a bit like the man with his head in the oven and his feet in the refrigerator.

Finally, stable growth rates on both sides of the Atlantic are desirable. If that means somewhat higher exchange rate volatility, that is a reasonable trade-off since hedging and other techniques are available. One, however, does not necessarily follow the other—stability and prosperity depend on the policies of the countries themselves. Given the interdependence of Europe and the United States, as much harmonization and coordination as possible would be highly desirable. The idea of decoupling what are already two quite, though not totally, separate economies into more discrete camps will prove deleterious to both.

It is important that Europe remain strong, stable, and serene. Much has been accomplished over the past fifty years to advance this cause, and continued effort should not be spared. I hope the day will come when the Euro takes its place with the dollar and yen as undoubted money. The political decisions to accomplish that objective successfully are Europe's, and Europe's alone, to make.

Liberalism and Illiberalism in the New Europe

Brian Hindley

Reader, Department of Economics, London School of Economics

"Tories Embarrassed by European Allies," said a headline in the *Times* (December 8, 1993) in the run-up to the 1994 elections for the European Parliament. The embarrassment is due to the draft manifesto of the European People's Party, with whom British Conservatives (a k a Tories) normally vote in the European Parliament. One sentence is enough to convey the flavor of the manifesto and to explain conservative embarrassment. It says that "governments must ensure that the functioning of the market remains subordinate to the general welfare and social justice."

That free markets are better for the general welfare than are political processes is, of course, the central proposition of classical liberal thought. British Conservatives (and Republicans in the United States) sometimes wobble in their application of it. Few of them, though, would deny its force or fail at least to pay it lip service. The failure of their European counterparts to offer even lip service reveals an intellectual gulf. The future of European trade policy—and almost everything else in the European Union—depends on the side of it that Europe chooses.

Maastricht had no direct bearing on trade policy issues. Trade policy, though, reflects the polity deploying it, and Maastricht was a skirmish in the struggle over the future character of the European Union. The federalist treaty struggling to emerge did not quite make it.

Debate about Liberalism

But debate in the EU is not just about—or even most importantly about—whether there should be a United States of Europe. It is also about liberalism. Many in the EU, and not only in Britain, suspect the EU of harboring illiberal, protectionist, and statist tendencies and are concerned that a United States of Europe would turn tendency into reality. Perhaps that view places too much weight on the illiberal, protectionist, and statist histories of most of the principal

21

national players in the EU. The conflict between liberalism and illiberalism is nevertheless real.

Continental Europeans and commissioners inveigh against "the Anglo-Saxon idea that the EU should be merely a glorified free trade area." And, of course, an area in which voluntary transactions can proceed without official restrictions is exactly what liberals *do* want. Liberals respond: "Why *merely* free trade? What larger enterprise do the federalists have in view? What do they want a federal United States of Europe *for*?"

Federalists dismiss such questions as nit-picking. They command the prevailing political current, at least among the Continental elites, which is what seems to count in the emerging Europe. They do not feel obliged to offer more than clichés.

The leading cliché is that a federal EU is "necessary to ensure peace between France and Germany." But the idea that war between France and Germany is a threat of such magnitude that it should dominate current policy is surely loony, and the proposition that only a federal Europe can avert it is plainly ridiculous. Americans know that parts of a federation can go to war with one another.

Another cliché points to the benefits of cooperation. But while it may be true that the European nations can gain much from cooperation, that fact alone cannot make a case for federation. In the European context, *federalism* means providing legal means for the coercion of one member-state by others. But if cooperation will yield benefits, why is coercion needed? Cooperation in the defense of Western Europe yielded great benefits, for example, but did not require a federal Europe.

The Need for Federation

The one reason for wanting a federal Europe that starts to make sense, however, does little to quell concerns about the potential for illiberality of a United States of Europe. It appears in calls for a Europe that can "deal on equal terms with the United States and Japan." No single European state can any longer play a leading role on the world stage, the argument goes, but a union of European states *will* have that capacity.

The typical inclusion in the formula of Japan suggests that economic relations are seen as the problem. Yet what problem? In matters of trade, the EU already acts as a single unit and can and does deal on equal terms with the United States and Japan.

French farmers might wearily reflect, as they block autoroutes to demonstrate against the General Agreement on Tariffs and Trade, or overturn lorries bringing meat or fruit into France, that their lives would be easier if a united Europe backed the Common Agricultural Policy (CAP). But such pipe dreams cannot be separated from the issue of liberality. What arrangements might be thrust on the EU that a United States of Europe could avoid *and* that would be in the interests of its citizens to avoid? Or is a United States of Europe attractive because it would have the power to thrust on others arrangements that the EU could not?

It may be convenient for a U.S. president to pick up the telephone to talk to his counterpart in Europe. The conversation, though, may not be worth the trouble. It may be convenient to return to a United States of Europe the responsibility for order on "its" area. But the order might not be exactly what the United States had in mind.

Even if the federal project fails, the future course of European trade policy is obscure. The European socioeconomic system—expensive welfare benefits financed in part by employers—cries out for revision, with unemployment high and rising across the Continental EU. But the EU might try to defend it. That would almost certainly entail an increase in barriers to imports, which are widely and erroneously held to be at the root of the problem.

The European socioeconomic system is a symbol of European distinctiveness, and symbolic reassurance that Europe exists is important to the EU elites. Like *nouveaux riches,* they seek ways of telling the world that they have arrived—even if they have not, quite.

Past symbols of Europe have been pretty disastrous—and the European socioeconomic system fits well with a tradition that started with the CAP. One of the few hopeful things to emerge from Maastricht, indeed, is the prospect of a symbol that is in principle not damaging. The single currency does not have much going for it in the way of economics, but if it provides enough symbolic weight to keep the federalists from tampering with everything else to which they might attach a symbolic value, it could be worth its weight in gold.

Americans would be foolish to bet on that happening, though. Hope for the other thing, but if anyone offers you even odds, bet on a Europe in 2016 that is illiberal, protectionist, and statist.

Don't "Euro-nize" the Union!

HEINZ A. J. KERN

Professor, Department of International Relations, Boston University

Economic and monetary union is the most ambitious common policy the members of the European Union have ever sought to realize. Their national currencies are being socialized into the Euro. If successful, that union would also mean the most critical loss of sovereignty for the EU states.

EU demagogues proclaim that not only the future of integration but also the peace and well-being of the entire continent hinge on the successful implementation of European Monetary Union. They portray EMU as another essential integration step by arguing that a single market necessitates a single currency, that no country could determine its own monetary policy any longer, that a single currency helps fend off Europe's American and Japanese competitors, and that all participating countries would benefit. German advocates of EMU not only agree but also project the belief that the Euro will be at least as stable as the deutsche mark.

This conviction has created an atmosphere of inevitability about economic union, and the pressures of making or breaking the community are mounting. Thus, the European Union's credo: EMU at any price. But these are only pretenses. The major purpose of the EMU is to curtail Germany's monetary and economic power. Such constraints on the German economy would be to the detriment of the whole of Europe.

The Power Politics behind EMU

Jacques Delors, when president of the EC Commission, declared that the EMU is a tool for breaking the monetary hegemony of the Bundesbank. Many other EU governments share his notion that the suffering at the hands of the Bundesbank "butchers" in the European Monetary System (EMS) "slaughterhouse" has to end. French politicians stated that "France will regain its sovereignty only when Germany gives up the deutsche mark." Germany's "closest" friend "accepted sharing our [French] monetary sovereignty in order that we not submit to that of others." Yes, claims *Le Monde* emphatically and with good reason, Maastricht is a second Versailles for Germany—and the price it has to pay for unification.

The German government could not agree more with the French-led castration attempt at its economic well-being. High government officials concurred that the EMS is, in essence, a German system and "cannot be a permanent solution for Europe's monetary arrangements. In the long run, it is unacceptable for other members to have to acquiesce in monetary decisions made by the Bundesbank." Former German chancellors demanded that Germany give up the deutsche mark before being able to enjoy the benefits of this strongest of currencies so much that they would not want to give it up.

All this sounds like the functionalists' plan to install a technocracy in Brussels that possesses the only and the true solution to any problem. Politics and power, as forces of evil, will allegedly be dispelled. The EMU and the Euro have been chosen as the saviors of Europe's monetary relations. The optimal and only solution has been found for each country and the entire European Union! Why bother then about some flaws in its construction design?

The Four Major Errors of the EMU

The initial flaw of the EMU stipulations in the Maastricht Treaty is to ignore the imperative of accomplishing economic convergence first. Ideally, national economies first need to grow closer together in performance (that is, growth, productivity, trade, and investment), economic structures, and macroeconomic policies to withstand external shocks and crises before monetary union can even be contemplated. Economic divergence, rather than convergence, however, is the reality among the fifteen member-countries today.

Monetary convergence should not be confused with economic convergence. Similar interest and inflation rates, for example, do not necessarily generate similar growth and productivity increases.

Since this kind of economic convergence is rarely accomplished, a second-best solution for the realization of monetary union would be market structures flexible enough to respond to disequilibrium. Labor and capital mobility, however essential for avoiding misallocation of resources, is low in Western Europe. Currently, only about 1 percent of the entire EU work force is employed in other EU countries. This immobility cannot be compensated for by downward flexible wages because of the considerable wage rigidities in the union.

Different cultural traditions, qualifications, and multiple language barriers greatly hamper factor mobility in Europe.

The second decisive shortcoming of the EMU portion of the treaty is to underestimate the importance of common economic policies. Lack of common policies, in turn, leaves all such matters in the domain of the nation-states. Quite understandably, the states have not shown a willingness to give up sovereignty over their sources of revenue. The asymmetry between monetary and economic policies is further accentuated by the need to maintain different economic policies, taking into consideration the specific conditions in the respective states—not to mention the different views regarding the efficiency of free markets and the benefits of interventionist measures. Furthermore, those who argue in favor of a supply-side course of action should remember how quickly the pendulum can swing back to inflationary demand-management strategies. In this vein, one should not be blinded by tough talk—even the Italians have argued for greater wage flexibility "à la USA"—and weak actions: real wage increases are still higher than productivity gains in the majority of EU countries.

The German Bundesbank has argued all along that a strict monetary policy alone cannot provide stability. Under EMU, income, growth, cyclical, tax, and social policies take on pivotal importance because the exchange rate mechanism does not exist anymore to help the domestic economy adjust in times of crises. Wage increases have to be matched by productivity gains. Since real wage decreases are not likely to occur in Western Europe, the potentially crisis-ridden countries are likely to counter unemployment with fiscal policies leading to higher debt and thus inflation.

In a strict monetary union, the crisis could no longer be "resolved" by printing more money. A monetary union, though, would abolish the obstacle of continued borrowing by eliminating the exchange rate risk and lowering the interest rate–increasing effect of national budgets. The unpleasant result could be that the other member-states would have to bear the consequences in the form of higher interest rates caused by those fiscally irresponsible players.

A common currency would also make wage differentials much more transparent. Given the vastly different conditions among the EU member-states and the countries' record of instability, the EMU will most likely lead to a leveling of wage differentials. That leveling will be fostered by the European Union's pledge to harmonize the living conditions of its members. Conversely, this leveling of incomes is not likely to be matched by productivity increases in the weaker countries.

Therefore, the Bundesbank has pleaded desperately to permit only those countries displaying a certain "culture of stability" to advance to the EMU. The president of the Bundesbank, Hans Tietmeyer, has pointed out that stability-conforming policies have not taken root in the European Union as of yet.

It is no surprise that the Maastricht Treaty is somewhat elusive about the necessity to pursue such long-term stability-oriented monetary and economic policies in accordance with the Maastricht criteria—the third major defect in the EMU construct. The criteria are depicted as one-time deadlines rather than permanent economic goals—now to be remedied by a so-called stability pact to which all agree in principle but resist in terms of concrete commitments. The true relevance of the criteria, however, should lie in ensuring that only healthy economies can enter the EMU to avoid burdening other participants with their economic woes.

Right now, of all the members, only Luxembourg meets all the criteria. The EU's debt-to-GDP ratio increased from 56 percent to 71 percent between 1991 and 1995. Only recently have measures—albeit haphazard—been undertaken to curb the national public deficits, mostly through tax increases instead of real budget cuts. The EMU candidates have had six years to improve their stability records but without avail. Even for countries like Italy and Belgium, realistic estimates show that meeting the criteria would have been possible only had they started in time to implement modest austerity programs.

If the entrance hurdle is too high, why not simply lower it? Belgium and Italy have already attempted to relax the Maastricht criteria by invoking the "Irish example." In 1994, the EC Commission set a negative precedent by deciding that Ireland, which needed seven years to reduce its debt-to-GDP ratio from 116 to 93 percent, met the budget criterion without coming close to the reference value of 60 percent, as required by the Maastricht Treaty. Another notion is that the criteria should be ignored altogether because the de facto currency union between Belgium and Luxembourg functions quite well despite Belgium's debt-to-GDP ratio of more than 140 percent! But who else can claim Belgium's high savings rate?

The Maastricht Treaty could also be watered down by allowing the members simply to usher themselves into the EMU by majority vote in the EU Council once they have determined their readiness to join. In recommendations to the council, the EC Commission and the European Monetary Institute are obliged to take into account such elusive factors as "the results of the integration of the markets" and "the development of unit labor costs." In other words, there are plenty of reasons for a "softer" interpretation of the criteria.

Indeed, the hope for an independent European Central Bank with a strict monetary policy has become the last line of defense. The fourth major error in the EMU scheme is the belief in the independence of the ECB and its ability to impose strict monetary policies. While the EU members agree on the importance of monetary policy, they disagree fundamentally on the necessity of pursuing monetarist policies Bundesbank-style. Many countries see monetary stability as one of many goals—such as the reduction of unemployment and the strengthening of economic growth—monetary policies have to satisfy. Consequently, quite a number of EU member-states' officials have already spoken out against the independent status and focus on price stability of the ECB.

Given this situation, economic policies that do not support stability could exert tremendous pressure on the ECB to accommodate the printing-press policies of the past. The ECB is not likely to display the courage necessary to resist. The no-bail-out clause stipulates only that the European Union should not be, rather than must not be, responsible for the debt of any national government. The interdependence of the single European market might create additional pressures. Insolvency might cause such strong ripple effects that other member-states would have to take action to avoid further damage. Even if the no-bail-out clause holds, the pressure to increase the European Union's structural and regional funds would be enormous. The accumulation of those funds would open the door to massive interstate financial transfers through which the failures of national economies could be equalized.

At this point, it is not certain that the member-banks of the ECB system will be "independent"; for example, interest-rate decisions in a number of countries are still contingent on governmental decision making. The Maastricht Treaty itself, although committed to ensuring price stability, does not quantify that goal, notwithstanding the fact that the price and interest sensitivity among the countries is vastly different. In addition, the Council of Ministers, not the ECB, will decide the exchange rate policy for the Euro.

The most important argument against the prospect of creating an ECB in the Bundesbank image comes from the member-countries' desire to escape the Bundesbank-dominated EMS system. The EMS made the weaker countries pay for their economic sins—and "imposed" greater stability than those countries ever had. As a result, they have to do the intervening borrowing and interest-rate raising when their currencies hit the limits of their exchange rate mechanism margins against the deutsche mark. Germany is the only country still running an autonomous monetary policy. Given the countries' apparent reluctance to bear the costs of economic stability in the future, a more democratized monetary policy would be a more lax one.

It is not only the different orientation of monetary policy but also the different financial habits and conditions in the member-states that will make it difficult to develop common monetary instruments, policies, and goals, which were neglected in the rush toward Maastricht. In terms of a common monetary policy, far-reaching differences still have to be overcome. The EU states have different traditions as well as divergent patterns of financial markets, including different tax laws. While Germany pursues a medium-term policy of money supply management for different monetary markets, England had to abandon that policy because of its "short-termism," thus coupling a stability-oriented money supply policy directly to the inflation rate. No monetary policy has emerged that could both reconcile these differences and satisfy the different market requirements.

Furthermore, currency unions need to react similarly to the policy instruments. In the European Union, however, interest rates affect the economies differently because of the varying structures of home ownership and industrial finance.

Life without the EMU

Undoubtedly, the European Union has reached the most critical juncture since its inception in 1958. The time is not right for the EMU; its price would be a mediocre currency. "Euro-nization" is a recipe for disaster.

Economic convergence is far off. A smaller union—comprising perhaps the Benelux, France, Germany, and Austria—does not make sense because it would be too small to be effective and would split the community (how should the others ever catch up?). To bank the whole enterprise on the stability-conforming behavior of the members is much too risky. Since the Bundesbank's "community of fate and solidarity" might never be achievable, the incantation of a political union remains hollow. Under these circumstances, a truly

European government would either have to pump money into economically distressed regions—or have to send troops. This is certainly not the kind of "political roof" for EMU the union should aspire to.

Plausible economic and national rationales are sacrificed on the alters of political expediency and German self-abnegation. The EMU can work if, and only if, Germany dutifully bears the impotence of castration. But how long can a country ignore its own national interests? Germany's "partners" want to shoot two birds with one stone: to escape the iron stability-imposing Bundesbank regime and to contain Germany economically. By blaming Germany for its controlling influence in the EMS, they reveal their unwillingness to implement sound economic policies. These countries have clearly understood that they would have the same qualms with the EMU as a stability-enforcing union as they have with the EMS now. Therefore, they are looking forward to a "democratically controlled" ECB and a monetary policy that would support a demand-management policy with all the inflationary consequences. With one difference: Germany would then have to pay for this union through financial transfers and a weaker currency.

Hence, the question of peace, war, and the EMU occurs in a much clearer light. In general, EU countries have benefited from Germany's control of the EMS in terms of growth and stability.

Oddly enough, though, those countries have called off the EMS bargain. The time has come not to ask what Germany can do for the union but to demand from its partners sacrifices in the interest of economic stability and peace in Europe. It is risky business to try to put Germany into the straitjacket of the EMU. Containing Germany could become a high-stakes game. Who would deny Germany the right not to feel encircled? When will it break out of the EMU?

German Unease about Union

HANS MARTIN KÖLLE

Writer, Finanz und Wirtschaft *(Zurich)*

Despite intense publicity efforts of the Bonn government and the European Union Commission in Brussels to promote the European

Monetary Union—scheduled to start in 1999 and to introduce a single currency, Euro—the uneasiness of the German population keeps increasing, as every public opinion poll shows. Those opposed to a single currency have nowhere to turn politically. Chancellor Helmut Kohl is using his full personal clout and political power to press ahead with the EMU. And the main opposition parties, the Social Democrats and the Greens, are just as committed to a single currency since they voted unanimously with the government coalition in favor of the Maastricht Treaty in February 1992. Its ratification was rushed through the Bonn Parliament in unseemly haste; any thorough public debate, which such a momentous decision would have called for, was carefully avoided, thereby laying the foundation for the current public mistrust.

Monetary Stability

Most Germans are watching the approach of the EMU with a mixture of disbelief and resignation. Wolfgang Schäuble, parliamentary whip of the Christian Democrats and the second most powerful figure after Chancellor Kohl, realistically expects resistance among the German population to stiffen as the changeover date draws nearer. But he insists that all EMU decisions will be carried out regardless. Clearly, many people still do not realize that their cherished deutsche mark will simply disappear within a few years. Others resent that the best and most solid money Germany ever had will have to be traded for a common European currency that will probably be more inflation prone than the deutsche mark. Although most Germans today are too young to have felt the trauma of hyperinflation that followed each world war, that experience has become part of the collective German memory. The last currency reform in 1948, painful as it was due to the loss of most savings, introduced the deutsche mark, and with it began Germany's rise from the ravages of war to prosperity, political stability, and peaceful integration into the Western world. Why give up a central element of this achievement?

Obviously, Bonn and Brussels will have to provide an answer to this anguished query and to face the main preoccupation in Germany, that of a loss of monetary stability. The official line, often repeated, is that the Euro will be just as stable as the deutsche mark. That still leaves the first question unanswered because people do not see much sense in having to give up an asset of proven value in exchange for something that is at best just as stable. Bonn and Brussels reply that, in many ways, the Euro will be better than a national currency. It will strengthen the Common Market as it provides a uniform monetary base for trade between member countries. Exchange rate risks will disappear, and transaction costs will be lower. Competition will intensify, to the benefit of consumers. Moreover, participating governments will forever lose the ability to finance budget deficits in their own currency, which they used to control, and this situation will close an opening for inflation.[1]

Convergence Criteria

These promises seem vague and uncertain to most people, including a majority of economists, despite official assurances that no risks will be taken with regard to the strength of the Euro. Guarantee one, according to the government, will be the future European Central Bank, fashioned after the Federal Reserve System and the Bundesbank. It is expected to be even more stability minded than its two models. Guarantee two is the so-called convergence criteria written into the Maastricht Treaty. They set up five benchmarks of financial and fiscal stability that a country must meet to qualify for membership in the EMU. The crucial year is 1997, when each country's performance will be examined. In early 1998, the EU Council will determine who measures up and who does not. This mechanism will ensure, it is claimed, that only countries with a proven record of financial probity will be allowed to enter the EMU, while the flighty and inflationary ones have to stay out, at least for the time being.

Chancellor Kohl and his cabinet members emphasize time and again that these convergence criteria will be applied "strictly" and "with the utmost rigor." In saying that, the government needs to keep in mind not only the lingering doubts among voters but also an October 1993 ruling of the German constitutional court that held Germany could enter only into an EMU that has proved to be stable by strictly honoring the convergence criteria.

At this point, developments have taken a critical turn. State-

---

1. Of the larger EU countries, only Germany has had a truly independent central bank, free of political interference. The bank's sole mandate has been to ensure monetary stability through tight control of the money supply. Other central banks had to follow the directives of their finance ministries. Only recently did the central banks of France (in May 1993) and of Italy (in January 1994) achieve independence, as required by the Maastricht Treaty.

ments underlining the firmness of the convergence criteria are beginning to sound hollow as all independent forecasts raise doubts about whether France or even Germany can meet them. Both countries had hoped for a strong economic recovery after the recession of 1994. Instead, they are experiencing extremely slow growth. Fiscal revenues are falling below expectations, and government efforts to cut expenditures and reduce deficits are running into stiff resistance from opposition groups and trade unions. The upshot is that France is unlikely to meet the deficit/gross domestic product ratio of 3 percent in 1997, and Germany will certainly overshoot the public debt/ GDP target of 60 percent.

If, true to the Bonn government's promise, the criteria were to be strictly applied, neither Germany nor France would qualify in 1997, and the EMU would turn into an absurdity with only Luxembourg meeting all the requirements. The German government's standard response to that prospect has been that "stability is more important than the timetable," as Chancellor Kohl put it. This seems to indicate a willingness to postpone the starting date for a few years instead of tampering with the convergence criteria.

But, more recently, the official emphasis has been on the need to meet both the timetable and the criteria. This approach may be wishful thinking, but it shows that those who called for postponement as the easy way out must have had second thoughts on closer reading of the Maastricht Treaty. The starting date is clearly stated, and there are no provisions for pushing it back. It follows that postponement is an option to be avoided, not only because it might induce some countries to relax their stabilization efforts, as many fear, but mainly because it would require formal renegotiations of the Maastricht Treaty in order to agree on a new starting date. And this seemingly simple amendment would certainly bring forth a host of additional urgent proposals to soften the treaty in other respects. In the end, negotiators might find themselves unable to put the complex package together again. The wise course of action seems to be: Let us not touch the treaty, or the EMU might fail altogether. (There are a few sneaky ways around that problem, but lawyers warn against them as they would constitute an abuse of certain clauses and would therefore seriously impair the integrity of the treaty.)

But then what? Decision makers in Bonn and Brussels find themselves in a deepening dilemma. Although the Maastricht Treaty does not specify the number or names of countries to be among the first-round members of the EMU, it would make little political sense to start it without Germany and France. But if they do not reach the criteria—and postponement is fraught with danger—does not the convergence criteria offer a way out after all? The treaty itself seems to allow some leeway as it permits an "excess over the reference values" if it is "only exceptional and temporary" and if it has diminished "substantially and continuously" (article 104 b). Euro strategists are looking with growing interest into these provisions with a view to a perfectly legal softening of the criteria. Even Karl-Heinz Wessel, president of the German bankers' association, now calls for "responsible" interpretation of the convergence criteria, no longer a "strict" one.

But once the EU starts down that road, skeptics fear, stability will fall by the wayside. It may seem acceptable to relax the reference values just enough to admit Germany and France. But what about other countries that are not quite so close or even way off? They will insist on the same lenient treatment, and, instead of an objective evaluation, we will probably see a political tug-of-war in 1998, when ministers have to determine EMU membership.[2] Criteria will not be reached, not even by the big countries. This will be unimportant because politics will win over statistics when the decisive moment comes" (front page editorial by Erik Izraelewicz, *Le Monde*, June 21, 1996). From the outset, the EMU may turn out to be a permissive "inflationary club" rather than the "community of stability" touted by Brussels and Bonn.

There will be a price to pay when that happens. Currency traders will react negatively to prospects of a weaker, inflation-ridden Euro, and wild currency movements are likely to shake the markets.[3] And German voters will note that a soft interpretation of the Maastricht rules has taken place—not their "strict application" as Chancellor Kohl has promised. Some will turn to the constitutional

---

2. "Certainly, the convergence criteria have their importance. That is why decisionmakers in Paris and Bonn will continue to undergo the ritual of confirming that they will succeed in reaching the criteria. But everyone knows that these criteria will not be reached, not even by the big countries. This will be unimportant because politics will win over statistics when the decisive moment comes." Front page editorial by Erik Izraelewicz, *Le Monde*, June 21, 1996.

3. "I too am quite convinced that any softening of the criteria would be ruthlessly penalized by the markets." Hans Tietmeyer, president of the Bundesbank, in a speech to the Foreign Exchange Traders Convention in Frankfurt, May 17, 1996.

court to file complaints that might hold up German entry. But many will feel that Kohl has broken his word and will think twice about voting for him again in the general elections of October 1998.

Political Problems and Economic Arrangements

ALLAN H. MELTZER

Visiting scholar, American Enterprise Institute

Proponents of European Monetary Union will be forced to choose soon among three undesirable outcomes. They can postpone the date for beginning the European system of central banking and for having a single currency. Or they can accept that all countries will not be members, at least not at first. Or they can weaken or waive the criteria for membership in the monetary union so that most of the countries can enter.

None of these choices is attractive. Skepticism about monetary union has increased as unemployment has mounted and budget deficits in principal countries, including Germany and France, have remained above the Maastricht criterion, a maximum of 3 percent of the gross domestic product. Delaying the starting date inevitably increases doubts about whether monetary union will ever occur.

The second alternative, excluding some countries at the start, although formerly declared unacceptable, is now considered an acceptable outcome. The hope is that the excluded countries will take the necessary actions to become members. One of the requirements for membership is a government debt to GDP ratio not greater than 60 percent. Italy is not likely to meet this standard within the lifetime of any living person. Belgium is doubtful also.

A main benefit of monetary union comes from the reduction in the volatility of prices of internationally traded goods and resources. This benefit depends on the number of countries in the union. If intra-union trade is a small part of total trade, a country will be free of uncertainty about exchange rates on only a small part of its trade and investment. For example, if the monetary union includes only the current deutsche mark bloc, then nearly two-thirds of exports from Denmark, France, and Germany would be with countries outside the monetary union.

The third alternative would waive the criteria for some countries. This seems the least desirable alternative because it relaxes fiscal discipline from the start. If countries are not required to follow the fiscal rules to gain admission, how likely are fiscal rules to be enforced after countries become members? Is Germany likely to expel France, if France has a large budget deficit? How can rules be applied to any country if they do not apply to every country?

Questions such as these lay bare one of the three major flaws in the Maastricht plan—the rules can be waived, and the enforcement mechanisms are vague or nonexistent. Vague enforcement mechanisms heighten uncertainty about how the system would work in practice.

Much of the reason for the uncertainty lies in the different economic objectives that principal countries seek to achieve with monetary union. The Germans want to extend German rules for fiscal and monetary policy to the rest of Europe. They expect that, if their rules are adopted, currencies will be more stable and they will not be required to finance their neighbors' budget deficits. The French want to increase their influence over monetary policy. They chafe under rules made by the Bundesbank.

The second major flaw is that Germany and France have chosen an economic arrangement mainly to solve a perceived political problem. The problem, of course, is Franco-German relations. Lenders on both sides see value in establishing common institutions that will unite the two countries, replacing disparate ends with common purposes. The two countries are unable to get agreement on a federal structure, so they hope to move by steps toward monetary union.

As Otmar Issing, a director of the Bundesbank, has pointed out, they have reversed the usual process. Usually, political union precedes monetary union, for good reason. Control of government spending and budget finance is critical for effective monetary control over the long term. The current vague criteria for admission and weak enforcement of rules for budget discipline cannot substitute for a political mechanism. In the case of monetary union, the absence of a political arrangement to control deficits is particularly important because monetary union will increase pressures for regional transfers within Europe. The concern is that, in some future fiscal crisis, a country will bargain for a bailout by the central bank in exchange for an increase in domestic taxation or a cut in government spending. Agreements of this kind are familiar from International Monetary Fund and World Bank adjustment programs. Uncertainty about how such issues will be resolved in practice adds to uncertainty about the properties of a European currency.

The third major flaw is the elimination of exchange rate changes as a means of adjusting for differences in regional experience. Countries experience differences in growth rates or differences in response to important external and internal events. Exchange rate changes between currencies work to adjust economies in different circumstances. The oil price changes of the 1970s are an example of an external change. An example of an internal change is the appreciation of the UK pound after the discovery of oil in the North Sea.

If exchange rates are fixed, as in a monetary union, some other means of adjustment must be found. The alternatives are (1) workers move from declining regions to expanding regions; (2) wages rise in the expanding region and fall in the declining region; and (3) the expanding regions make fiscal transfers to the declining regions.

Language and other cultural barriers severely reduce mobility between European countries for all but menial jobs. Social welfare policies limit the downward adjustment of wages. Unemployed workers have chosen to keep social benefits and continued unemployment rather than to accept wage reduction. They seem likely to continue to do so.

This leaves only two remaining choices for Europe—budget transfers and continued unemployment—if there is to be a single currency. Failure to reach political agreement and vague rules for fiscal discipline expose Europe to repeated conflicts about the size and sustainability of transfers from rich to poor regions and from expanding to declining regions.

An additional source of conflict arises from the opportunity for exchange rate adjustment by countries that do not join the union. These countries retain an adjustment mechanism that countries within the union forgo. The member countries will complain that the nonmembers use their exchange rate to "export unemployment"—that is, to adjust. There are already many complaints of this kind by French and German producers against British and Italian producers. Opportunities for friction and conflict seem unbounded if part of Europe goes to monetary union and the rest opts out. A partial monetary union will test both the fabric of monetary union and the rules for open trade in the current European Union.

Will the EMU Be Established by 1999?

MANFRED J. M. NEUMANN

*Director, Institute for International Economics,
University of Bonn*

Establishing the European Monetary Union (EMU) by 1999 is a great challenge to Europe. It will mean completing the framework of economic integration, and it is expected to pave the way toward the political unification of Europe. Only a few member-countries of the enlarged Community of Fifteen (EU-15), however, will be likely to fulfill the entry criteria set by the Maastricht Treaty of 1991.

On the State of Macroeconomic Convergence

The Maastricht Treaty requires that European Union (EU) countries converge to a comparable performance of macroeconomic stability. The degree of convergence is measured by four criteria: the rate of inflation, the long-term interest rate, the fiscal policy stance, and the stability of the exchange rate. According to the established timetable, the decisive convergence test will be conducted by March 1998. To qualify for participation, a country must have been fulfilling the first three criteria at least since 1997 and the exchange-rate criterion since March 1996.

The nominal convergence, as measured by the differences in national rates of inflation and in long-term interest rates, has developed favorably. The inflation criterion stipulates that a country's inflation rate not exceed the average of the three lowest inflation rates by more than 1.5 percentage points. Similarly, the long-term interest rate must not exceed the averaged interest rate level of the three countries with the lowest inflation by more than 2 percentage points. Since 1995 both criteria have been met by all member-countries except the four southern European countries—Greece, Italy, Portugal, and Spain.

The exchange rate criterion requires that a country's currency participate in the exchange rate mechanism of the European Monetary System for at least two years and not have been devalued; it must remain without major tensions within the "normal" exchange-rate band. There is a hidden political conflict concerning whether the current, wide band of plus or minus 15 percent or the former, narrow band of plus or minus 2.25 percent shall be identified as the normal band. As the Bundesbank has rightly pointed out, though, only the narrow band creates an informative test. Under this interpretation, only Germany, Austria, and the three Benelux countries qualify. Two currencies have been devalued; three currencies, including the French franc, have moved below the narrow band for at least eleven consecutive months; and another three currencies do not participate in the exchange rate mechanism at all.

The greatest obstacle to achieving the EMU by 1999 is the lack of fiscal convergence. Participation requires a solid state of public-budget finance. This is gauged by two measures: first, the deficit/gross domestic product ratio should not exceed, or at least should be close to, 3 percent, and second, the debt/GDP ratio should not exceed 60 percent or, if higher, should be falling markedly. By the end of 1996, the debt requirement was met by Germany, France, Luxembourg, and the United Kingdom. Of the remaining eleven countries, only Ireland achieved a marked fall of its debt ratio. Even worse is the performance with respect to the size of public deficits. The 3 percent mark was violated by twelve countries, notably by the larger countries: Germany (4 percent), France (4 percent), and Italy (6.6 percent).

Summing up, at present only one country meets all the convergence criteria: Luxembourg. To be sure, the present state does not count. In assessing the probability that the EMU will start on time, we have to consider that the governments of most EU countries are currently reviewing their spending programs, notably the expenditures on social security, in search of sufficiently large spending cuts that promise to meet the fiscal criteria in 1997.

If Early EMU, Then Which Countries?

It is too early to draw a definite conclusion about the final outcome of this continuing process. Yet it would be wishful thinking to believe that many countries will be able to improve fiscal performance sufficiently to qualify for early EMU. Much depends on whether economic growth will pick up. While redressing the government sector is conducive to stronger economic growth in the long run, it is likely to weaken aggregate demand initially.

In any case, under the most optimistic scenario, Germany, France, Austria, Ireland, and the three Benelux countries may form the starting group (Denmark has decided not to join initially). This scenario rests on the probably unrealistic assumption that Austria, Belgium, and the Netherlands will succeed in reducing their debt ratios significantly and that France will strongly cut into the deficit that currently runs at 4 percent of GDP.

There is no doubt that the EMU will be realized, should this or a similar group qualify, provided it includes Germany and France. In this case, a large political payoff is expected from the French-German advance toward full-fledged economic and monetary union. According to the official view, the replacement of national currencies by the new currency, termed "Euro," will also provide sizable economic gains from saving on money-changing and hedging costs. Those gains will hardly be large, however, even though two-thirds of this group's European trade is within-group trade. Most companies do not find it worthwhile to hedge trade transactions among Germany, Austria, and the three Benelux countries, given the stable exchange rates in this region.

Moreover, such gains may easily be consumed by a loss of competitiveness vis-à-vis the rest of the EU-15. The official split of the community between a fast-moving EMU-group and the remaining weak-currency countries is likely to induce a wave of speculation against the latter in 1998. This would negatively affect one-third of the EMU group's trade within Europe. The export industries of France and Ireland would be hit the most, given that 50 percent of their European trade is with EU countries outside the EMU group.

But note that the optimistic assumption of an early EMU group that includes France is much in doubt. To date, the efforts of the French government to redress spending have not been successful. In autumn 1995, the French government announced its intent to reduce the deficit of the social security budget from last year's 65 billion to 17 billion French francs this year. Recent estimates, however, indicate that the deficit will not fall below 40 billion francs. As a result, the total deficit ratio targeted for this year at 4 percent is not likely to be reached.

Options If France Fails to Qualify

An EMU without France does not promise any economic net gains. More important from the German point of view, it would jeopardize the whole European enterprise of economic and political integration. In all likelihood, the strong political alliance between France and Germany, to date the driving force of European integration, would seriously suffer. Therefore, the German government will have to consider the following options: a weakening of the convergence criteria or the postponement of EMU.

To take the first option is a risky enterprise for the Kohl government. Opinion polls indicate that a majority of Germans prefer to keep the deutsche mark. For this reason, the Kohl government has always promised Germans that it will insist on a strict application of the convergence criteria in order to make sure that the unpopular Euro will be as stable as the mark. To retreat from the promise will be to invite political defeat in the election year 1998. Consequently, if France fails to qualify, the EMU will have to be postponed. A conceivable approach is to postpone the EMU for three years, to reaffirm the commitment of continuing the process of fiscal consolidation, and possibly to strengthen enforcement by suitable sanctions. One will not have to wait until 1998 to assess whether postponement is necessary. In any case, it is not likely that either France or Germany will wish to take the official initiative. Rather, they will prefer a third country, such as Italy, to put forward the proposal.

Variable Geometry in Europe

MICHAEL SPICER
Member of Parliament (Britain)

What Variable Geometry Means

Variable geometry has suddenly become a term much used—and perhaps as a consequence—much abused. It is important to be clear about what it actually means. It does not, for instance, mean the breakup of the European Union. On the contrary, it provides the means by which the European Union can move forward in a stable and harmonious manner, that is, with the consent of its people. Variable geometry rests on two assumptions: first, that the nations of Europe have differing features and aspirations, and second, that they have a mutual desire to cooperate as closely as they can, above all on matters of trade.

Variable geometry permits members of the European Union to choose which areas of policy to place under EU jurisdiction, which to treat as matters for intergovernmental cooperation within EU structures, and which to retain under wholly national control.

Variable geometry allows countries to collaborate in their own way on matters of mutual interest within the context of a European single market. Some, for example, might want to adopt a common foreign and security policy; others, a common asylum and immigration policy; others, a common monetary policy or a common fisheries policy. In each case, the degree to which a country chose to amalgamate its policies would be decided democratically by the voters of that country. Europe would, in effect, coalesce into a set of overlapping circles.

A number of policies currently under the control of Brussels would, on the basis of variable geometry, be areas that some member-states might choose to reclaim. The basic rule should be as follows: member-states should be free to administer for themselves any policy that cannot be shown directly to affect the internal affairs of another member. Thus, Brussels would still have jurisdiction over matters such as the internal market and cross-border environmental pollution. But, in other areas, member-states would not be obliged to subordinate their policies to the European Union. They may well choose to do so, but they would not be forced to.

A More Flexible Framework

Elements of variable geometry are already working in practice. The Schengen agreement on open borders, for example, exists within the EU but covers only nine of fifteen members. Greece never participated in the European Monetary System. Britain and Denmark are not obliged to move to stage three of monetary union. But the most important precedent of all is the protocol on social policy agreed at Maastricht. This allows some member-states "recourse to the institutions, procedures and mechanisms of the treaty" without extending to all member-states.

This principle should be developed. Instead of an ad hoc series of opt-outs, what is required is a major treaty revision to allow for flexible integration within the framework of a single market. Opponents of this model call it à la carte and complain that it would be unworkable. But in reality it is the current model that is unworkable. Forcing countries to pursue a common policy, regardless of whether it is in their interest, creates far greater instability. Uniformity cannot be an end in itself.

Variable geometry is an idea whose time is coming. For two years now, I have led the European Research Group, which brings together members of parliament from all over Europe who support this model. Its members are deputies and senators from no fewer than thirty-five center-right parties in twenty-four countries. At a seminal meeting at Brasenose College, Oxford, in 1994 and later meetings at Paris and Brussels, we agreed on a radical program based on variable geometry and, where a nation wished, on the restoration of power to national parliaments.

Three Factors

Three factors make variable geometry a pressing and desirable objective: the pressure of enlargement, the need to address legitimate public concerns about the European Union, and the need to achieve a successful outcome to the Intergovernmental Conference.

Eastward enlargement presents the European Union with the greatest challenge since its foundation. For fifty years, the historic kingdoms of Central and Eastern Europe were cut off from normal political development, frozen out of the European civilization that had been their heritage. If the European ideal means anything at all, it must mean healing the division of our continent. I share the frustration of many of the negotiators from the former Soviet bloc countries when they hear EU officials speaking of a "common European home" while at the same time pursuing policies that will make enlargement quite impossible.

Institutions designed for six similar Western European economies recovering from the Second World War will not be able to administer Europe effectively in all its diversity. Expansion will bring an unprecedented variety of conditions within EU jurisdiction. It will simply not be practical to apply uniform policies to so many members, regardless of their needs.

Who can seriously imagine that the common agricultural policy could apply in its present form to Poland or Ukraine? Or that Slovak or Romanian employers could accept the social charter? Or that the structural and cohesion funds could be extended to Lithuania or Bulgaria? Above all, can anyone imagine the applicant countries' being able to participate in monetary union under the proposed terms?

The only solution is to allow the applicant countries to retain control over a number of policy areas while participating in the single market. It must be made possible for the Central and Eastern European states to participate in the European Union without accepting the full burden of the so-called *acquis communautaire*. Once this principle has been established for the sake of the new applicants, it will have to apply to the existing members.

Almost as pressing as enlargement is the need to address the widespread disenchantment of citizens currently inside the European Union. Forcing different countries to adopt uniform policies after a majority vote cannot be in the long-term common interest. It will necessarily result in some or all states adopting policies that are less suited to their circumstances than those that they would have chosen for themselves.

So, for example, a common European monetary policy, in the shape of the European exchange rate mechanism (ERM), forced many members to pursue policies that ran wholly contrary to their economic needs: in Britain, interest rates rose to 15 percent during a deep recession; in France, 10 percent real interest rates were combined with 10 percent unemployment; in Spain, the peseta was overvalued despite 25 percent unemployment. Similar effects were felt in Denmark, Ireland, Portugal, and Italy. Germany, by contrast, arguably suffered from lower interest rates than domestic conditions required, as the Bundesbank, with much grumbling, bowed to political pressure to keep the ERM up and running.

The ERM illustrated in microcosm what is wrong with squeezing diverse countries into uniform policies: everyone lost and no one gained. The same effect can be seen across the range of European Union activities, whether in trade, agriculture, fisheries, or social policy.

As a result, people are increasingly turning against the very concept of nations coming closer in Europe. The past four years have seen an unprecedented rise in public hostility to the European Union, as people suffer from the effects of common policies. The list of discontented groups grows by the day: British dairy farmers impoverished by the quota system and now crippled by the beef export ban; French fishermen rioting against the common fisheries policy; Portuguese part makers hampered by intrusive and unnecessary health and safety directives; German taxpayers burdened by the spiraling EU budget; Spaniards thrown out of work by the Maastricht criteria. In each of these cases, people are beginning to react against a system that disregards their own needs to pursue harmonization as an end in itself.

The way to address their concerns is through variable geometry, to allow countries to administer for themselves matters that are of wholly domestic concern.

The third factor, and most immediate, relates to the Intergovernmental Conference. Under present arrangements, the positions that the various governments have adopted at the Intergovernmental Conference offer little prospect of an eventual agreement. At one extreme, Germany, Italy, and the Benelux states are calling for political union: more powers for the European Parliament; an erosion of the national veto; common policies in the fields of foreign affairs, defense, immigration, and law; and an end to the intergovernmental elements of Maastricht. At the other, the British government has pledged to resist any such moves and is now indicating that it may seek to repatriate power in some areas.

These two positions are, on the surface, irreconcilable. But variable geometry offers a way through by allowing each country to fulfill its own ambitions within a free trade area. Thus, some countries may wish to confine their economies, even their governments, while others may wish to remain in a free trade area and no more. In either case, they should be allowed to do so.

Any change to the Maastricht Treaty, under article N, requires the unanimous support of all member-states. If Germany and the Benelux states, for example, wish to go ahead on their own with full political and economic union, they need Britain's permission. The position of the British government should be that that permission will be granted only if Britain and other countries are similarly granted permission to repatriate power from Brussels.

A Multifaceted Europe

Variable geometry thus offers every country the opportunity to come away from the Intergovernmental Conference with what it wants. It will prevent the negotiations from breaking down in a welter of acrimony and veto. The extent to which any country integrated its policies would be determined by its interests and the wishes of its electors. It is wrong to see this model in terms of inner tiers and outer tiers. What is emerging is a multifaceted Europe with as many tiers as there are member-states.

Nothing could be more in keeping with the tradition of European civilization. The one fact that has distinguished Europe through-out its history has been that it has always remained a diverse plural-ity of nation-states. The great civilizations of the East all became centralized as monolithic empires: the Ming Empire, the Mogul Em-pire, the Ottoman Empire. They became overtaxed, bureaucratized, standardized, and introverted and plunged, as a result, into eco-nomic decline. Europe, by contrast, fostered the values of freedom and enterprise, of diversity and variety. These values, transplanted also to the western shores of the Atlantic, have been Europe's strength. To ignore them now would be a betrayal of the European heritage.

Burdens of the Welfare State

IRWIN STELZER
Director, regulatory policy studies, American Enterprise Institute

Americans have a lot to think about. Oldsters are being told that the system of national health insurance on which they have come to depend will soon be bankrupt, leaving them to face a mounting pile of doctors' bills with less and less help from the government. Young-sters are being told that the social security system that has made it possible for retirees to live with a modicum of dignity will not be there for them, as fewer and fewer working-age people will be called on to support more and more longer-living elderly citizens. Work-ers are being told that they can no longer look to their corporate employers for long-term ensured employment or for generous ben-efits. And nonworkers, those now receiving government assistance of all kinds, are being told that such aid will be distributed less freely in the future, as the nation gropes for ways to reform its welfare state.

Greater Problems in Europe

With all these worries on their minds, it is difficult to persuade Americans to pay much attention to the even greater problems afflicting welfare states in France, Germany, and other European countries—or to care whether an increasingly sclerotic Europe can solve its problems and once again put its economies on the path to noninflationary economic growth. Much as the street gang in *West Side Story* told the befuddled Officer Krupke that "we've got troubles of our own," Americans are, by their lack of interest, telling Europeans that our country has big problems to solve, so big that it has neither the time nor the resources to devote to economic problems on the other side of the Atlantic—unless, of course, those are problems of the former Soviet Union, whose nuclear arsenal and continuing flirtation with the good old days of the cold war somehow manage to pry the odd billion out of otherwise grudging Americans.

This lack of concern with Europe's problems may well be a mistake. Just as America's ability to live in peace cannot be divorced from the maintenance of peace in Europe—like it or not, we now have 18,000 troops in the Balkan powder keg—so America's ability to live in prosperity cannot be divorced completely from economic circumstances in Europe. The European Union remains an important trading partner: in 1995, we sold $250 billion in goods and service to the countries of the EU, more than one-fourth of all our exports. The EU also cooperates, albeit sometimes reluctantly, with the United States in a host of economic programs, from maintaining a reserve of oil against the day when the Middle East's Arabs might unsheathe their oil weapon and initiate another boycott, to helping in cases of international financial fraud, to siding with America in its efforts to preserve a free trade regime (France is an exception in this regard, preferring *dirigiste* policies such as fixed exchange rates to what it variously calls "the law of the jungle" and "the anarchy of the marketplace").

It would be stretching a point to say that America's prosperity is inextricably tied to the economic well-being of Europe, but it would not be wrong to say that economic growth in America is far easier to maintain at a higher level if Europe prospers than if it sinks into more or less permanent recession. So we should care about Europe. And worry.

Burdens of the Welfare State

For if ever a region seems about to sink into a slough of economic despair and social upheaval, Europe is that place. The facts are quite

47

simple and widely agreed. With the possible but not certain exception of Great Britain, Europe's principal economies are groaning under the burden of their welfare states. France's government bureaucrats now claim more than half the country's gross domestic product, using some for purposes they deem wise—subsidizing an unprofitable airline (Air France), operating magnificently uneconomic trains—and redistributing the balance in a manner they consider just, after appropriate deductions for administrative costs.

Meanwhile, across the border, Germany's workers, once famous for their work ethic and efficiency, have used the economic clout of their trade unions and their political muscle to obtain lavish vacations, sick benefits so generous that it has become almost foolish to work on a Monday or Friday, and other fringes so costly that Germany's principal export has become jobs, as employers flee the country in search of the lower unit labor costs of Eastern Europe, Great Britain, and the United States.

Worse still, the European countries have made it so difficult to discharge employees that companies are extraordinarily reluctant to hire new workers. That, plus the huge ancillary costs associated with feeding the ravenous welfare states of Europe—even Great Britain's Conservative Party is devoted to its welfare state, with a Tory government defending the necessity of consuming 42 percent of all the goods and services Britons can produce—has generated levels of unemployment that may well threaten the future social stability of many European countries. In France, 12 percent of the work force is out of work; in Germany, one in ten of the country's workers cannot find jobs; in Spain, the unemployment rate is higher still, perhaps double those of its northern partners in the European Union. And in all these countries the number of long-term unemployed is high and rising.

Monetary Union

All this would be bad but acceptable were relief in sight. But any fair reading of the European situation leads to the conclusion that things are much more likely to get worse than they are to get better. Start with the drive toward monetary union, the replacement of individual national currencies with a single Eurocurrency. The Germans, determined to replace national sovereignty with a federal Europe, see such union as a giant step on the road to that federal Europe. Perhaps recognizing that Harvard professor Daniel Goldhagen's reading of the German national character in his *Hitler's Willing Executioners* is correct, Helmut Kohl says he wants to subordinate Germany to Europe, creating a European Germany. Some European (especially British) critics, of course, argue that he is seeking to accomplish with economic might what Germany never succeeded in accomplishing with military might, a German Europe.

No matter the motive, Kohl is Europe's most durable politician; Germany, even in its currently weakened state, its most powerful economy. Its citizens may not relish surrendering their stable deutsche mark for a currency to be managed jointly with the Portuguese, Spanish, Greeks, and Italians. And the Bundesbank inflation fighters may shudder at the thought of dealing with the French, who have vowed to subordinate the austere bankers to the more open-handed politicians on the board of the new European Central Bank. But Kohl pushes on, and monetary union appears likely to proceed, perhaps a bit behind schedule, perhaps with fewer members than originally anticipated, but proceed.

And therein lies a giant land mine in the path of Europe's move into the twenty-first century. For monetary union means compliance with the membership criteria set forth in the Maastricht Treaty, the most important being that national budget deficits cannot exceed 3 percent of the gross domestic product. To meet this standard, many European governments, most notably France and Germany, must either raise taxes or reduce outlays. The former is probably politically impossible in these already heavily taxed countries and, even if possible, would probably so slow growth as to be counterproductive.

Attacking the Welfare State

That leaves cutting expenditures, which means attacking the cherished welfare state—which brings us full circle. For it is the generous welfare state that makes it so expensive for employers to add workers; it is the generous welfare state that makes long-term unemployment a viable alternative to work; and it is the generous welfare state that dilutes workers' incentives to show up for work when mildly ill or merely with a felt need for a day off. Equally important, it is the generous welfare state that keeps budget deficits high, both by bloating expenditures and by stifling growth, thereby making tax cuts impossible—especially in countries in which self-financing, supply-side tax cuts are seen as a figment of the American imagination, implanted there by a second-rate movie actor who somehow became president.

It is this welfare state that Europe's politicians cannot attack. When the French leadership proposed relatively mild reforms, it found itself confronted with burning automobiles and riots in the streets of Paris, as cosseted public-sector workers shut the country down. The plain fact is that there is no support for market-based reforms in France.

The Communist-led CGT union, of course, has no use for markets. The elite that runs the country prefers its decisions to those of the market and is unprepared to cede control to impersonal market forces. The public-sector workers prefer the overmanned, underworked existence that has been theirs for as long as they can remember, and the more than 2 million civil servants promise to make a year-round affair of the winter of discontent if Prime Minister Alain Juppe carries out his threat to trim "layers of fat" from the government payroll. The heavily subsidized farmers have no intention of being forced to compete with more efficient American and Eastern European farmers. And the telecommunications and entertainment industry prefers protection from foreign competition, allegedly to preserve the nation's "culture," to producing programs and films that people want to see.

As for Germany, there is little hope that the current pressure of high unemployment and the exodus of jobs to more congenial climes will produce reforms drastic enough to allow Germany to break out of the economic trap in which it finds itself. Chancellor Kohl has proposed trimming his welfare state by, among other things, raising the retirement age for women from sixty to sixty-five, freezing child benefits, and reducing sickness benefits so that absenteeism pays only 80 percent as much as does work. He also wants to encourage employers to increase their hiring by making it somewhat easier for them to fire workers who prove either unsatisfactory or unnecessary, provoking criticisms of what is seen as his effort to convert Germany to an American-style hire-and-fire economy. Public-sector employees have taken to the streets, disrupting transport and mail delivery—a new style of confrontation that bodes ill for Germany's traditionally consensual labor-management relations.

Finally, Kohl wants to cut top rates of personal and corporate taxes, lower by a little the hated "solidarity tax" that has financed the reconstruction of eastern Germany, and scrap the 1 percent tax on personal wealth—the latter measure arousing the ire of the *Länder* (federal states), which depend on the revenues from that tax.

It is difficult to tell just how successful the not-to-be-underestimated chancellor will be in pushing through his "program for more growth and employment." But even if he succeeds, the reforms, which are by no means trivial (Kohl's proposed spending reductions come to 2 percent of GDP), are so limited that Germany will remain the high-cost producer in many of the markets in which it must compete. That, at least, is the view of Kurt Biedenkopf, the Christian Democratic governor of Saxony, and Gerhard Schröder, the Social Democratic governor of Lower Saxony, who argue that Germany's pay-as-you-go welfare system must be scrapped if the costs borne by employed workers are to be reduced sufficiently to make Germany competitive in world markets. Significantly, even these two reformers, more radical by far than Kohl, make it clear that they are not espousing the American way for Germany. Free markets are not for everyone, and the hunt for that elusive third way remains a European sport.

Given its current cost structure, Germany's entry into monetary union with its European partners could prove an extremely costly exercise. At the moment, Germany's high costs have made its products difficult to sell overseas. Even if those costs are trimmed a bit in the next few years, Germany is most likely to remain noncompetitive when the time for a switch to a single currency rolls around. Monetary union will lock into place the relationship of the mark to other currencies, preventing the mark from drifting down to make the price of German goods in overseas markets competitive with the prices of its rivals. Unless the rest of Europe adopts highly inflationary policies—unlikely if the European Central Bank holds its members to high standards of fiscal rectitude—Germany will be forced to accept sustained levels of high unemployment or make draconian cuts in its production costs by forcing workers to accept lower real wages and skimpier welfare benefits. No one can predict whether German society can withstand the strains such policies would produce or whether the costs would be worth the benefits Kohl perceives in subordinating Germany to a federal Europe.

Consequences for America

Americans should not delude themselves into thinking that none of this will have consequences here. French and German governments faced with persistent double-digit unemployment will look unfavorably on what they will see as job-destroying imports. Protectionist measures designed to keep American agricultural products, computers, telecommunications equipment, and other goods and services out of Europe will almost certainly follow. So, too, will stepped-up efforts to bar goods from Asia, forcing China, Japan, and other Asian countries to redouble their efforts to capture a greater share of America's markets, just when this country's trade balance will be deteriorating because of foreclosure from access to a united Europe's 370 million consumers.

An unlovely scenario. And one that American policy makers blithely ignore as they encourage Europe's nation-states to submerge themselves in a centralized, federal Europe, in the vain hope that a United States of Europe will be just like the United States of America—free-trading, free-market oriented, driven to full employment by the efforts of relatively low-taxed entrepreneurs operating in flexible labor and product markets. It will not.

The Euro Will Be Stable: An Interview with Norbert Walter

(Norbert Walter is the chief economist, Deutsche Bank Group.)

QUESTION: In mid-December 1995, the member-states of the European Union agreed on the name *Euro* for the future currency; this represented yet another step forward in achieving currency union. What do you consider the advantages of this currency union, which, on New Year's Day 1999, will herald a new era for Europe?

MR. WALTER: The obvious things first. Costs related to exchange will fall by the wayside. We Germans, for example, will be able to go out to dinner in Strasbourg without first having to exchange money and pay a fee for doing so. But the second and more important case to be made is that monetary transactions within Europe will become less

Reprinted from *Deutschland*, no.1, February 1996, with permission from the Press and Information Office of the Federal Government of Germany.

expensive and simpler to conduct—as is the case today with such transactions in a domestic setting. But for investment and long-term capital commitments, there is yet another factor even more important than the two arguments I have already mentioned: insecurity about future exchange rates will disappear. Experience has shown that this situation will lead to the investment of money in places where it makes sense, rather than in places with which we are familiar.

This shift should guarantee that in the economic process we Europeans will become more efficient, more competitive, and that our business once again will have a real chance in the competitive struggle with firms from North America and Southeast Asia.

QUESTION: At the same time, Europe will then represent a financial market as sizable as that in the United States. Surely that will also be attractive to investors.

MR. WALTER: Exactly. European markets will then be as good as their counterparts in North America and Japan. And that will, of course, help to get investors excited about this market, investors who so far have said that this market was simply too small for them.

QUESTION: Can you provide an example?

MR. WALTER: Look at the Central Bank of Singapore. Experience shows that it has a lot of money to invest. But when it invests money in a small market and later wants its money back, the bank often has to sell such a large amount that the value of that security drops very quickly. So the bank finds itself in a sort of mousetrap: when it wants to get out of some investment, the trap springs. Such a risk does not exist in a market as broad and deep as that in North America, and neither would it exist in a larger European financial market.

QUESTION: If a popular referendum were held on the issue in Germany today, the overwhelming majority of people would probably vote against the Euro and for keeping the deutsche mark. How do you explain that? Or which argument would you use to present the case in favor of the new currency?

MR. WALTER: We will get the population to reassess its view only if we make it clear to people that the new currency will be as stable and even more usable than the present excellent currency, the deutsche mark. Of course, many things can contribute to making the issue clearer. But it is also quite apparent that when Germans think about an exchange of money, they always associate it with the concept of currency reform. And in Germany—twice in this century, not long after both world wars—currency reform meant that you lost most of your financial wealth. This idea is completely off base when it comes to the European currency. But, in their heart of hearts, the Germans simply do not believe that. And as far as I am concerned, only one thing will help in overcoming this state of affairs: action by the most credible institution in Germany, the Bundesbank.

QUESTION: In which form?

MR. WALTER: The Bundesbank is the institution that at some point, at the latest in the course of 1997 but probably earlier, will help in removing the fears of citizens in Germany.

QUESTION: You said that the new currency will be more stable and better to use. I understand what you mean by the latter, but what is your description of *more stable*?

MR. WALTER: *Stability* in this sense means a low rate of inflation.

QUESTION: And will that be the case?

MR. WALTER: That will be the case. Five of our partner countries already have inflation rates today below 2 percent. When the Maastricht Treaty was signed in 1991, critics talked a blue streak about the treaty's mediocre requirements on stability. They now have to admit that the stability that has come about is surprisingly great. And all of this definitely had something to do with the Maastricht process.

QUESTION: Are these fears about the new currency a purely German phenomenon?

MR. WALTER: A few other countries are also worried about the new currency. Obviously, the Danes are not yet convinced that they need this European money. But in many countries such fears have different grounds. Many worry about losing their independence. Many Germans fear for the stability of their currency. The Mediterranean countries are saying that they finally want to have money that is worth something.

QUESTION: In France, you can still see some people counting in old francs, which have not existed for thirty years. To what do you attribute such a phenomenon, and how long will the Euro need to get out of people's pockets and find a place in their hearts?

MR. WALTER: The observations you mention about France show that money is obviously deeply rooted in the psyche and comes to be really accepted only when it has been established for a long time. As far as I am concerned, it would be nonsense to think that, come 1999, some great passion will break out for the Euro and everyone will begin to think in terms of Euros. That is simply unrealistic. Things will still be reckoned in national currencies for quite some time. When will the Euro become fully accepted? I think that is something we will have to ask our kids; my generation could not answer that question. We can introduce the Euro and help to make it valuable, but it will definitely take decades for it to get into children's books, so to speak.

QUESTION: At the beginning of 1998, the European Council will determine which countries have met the convergence criteria for currency union. So far that includes only Luxembourg. In your opinion, which countries will and should be included in the currency union?

MR. WALTER: The notion that currently only Luxembourg meets the Maastricht criteria is wrong. You have to bear in mind that the treaty is explicitly allowing for some leeway when it comes to interpreting the convergence criteria. This should, however, not be confused with "watering them down." Against this background, the Maastricht Treaty is quite clear. It states that those countries that fulfill the convergence criteria are included. The Maastricht Treaty does not specify, however, which countries will actually be included. But I cannot imagine that there will be a currency union that is not worthy of the name. Now, a currency union between Germany and Luxembourg is not included anywhere in the Maastricht Treaty, but I do not think this would be politically realistic. I do not think that a currency union will take place without France and Germany. I also think that if these two countries participate, there is a high probability that the Benelux countries and Austria will, too. That is not to say that, from today's point of view, all these countries will be able to surmount the remaining hurdles easily. To achieve all this, several of these countries, at least four, still have to undertake considerable efforts. Initially, the currency union will probably be made up of a group of about six countries.

QUESTION: When and in which way will the remaining countries enter the currency union? And further, won't classification bring about a two-speed Europe?

MR. WALTER: Europe has been a Europe of various speeds for quite a while already. Maybe the word *speed* is the wrong word because that makes it sound as if individual countries are moving in different categories. In reality, Europe is moving in various fields at varying speeds. When it comes to the North Atlantic Treaty Organization, for example, France was not even on the train for a long time but nevertheless played a leading role in the integration process. Apparently, some Europeans have doubts as to whether currency union is something important for them, whether they should be part of it from the beginning. But the only real question here is, Will countries be successful in fulfilling the criteria for entry? Some are also saying that even if and when they fulfill the criteria, they still will not want to be part of a currency union. So the issue for 1998 is different for different countries. For some of them, the fact of the matter is that they will not fulfill the convergence criteria at all, and they do not want to participate anyway. For others, failure to qualify might possibly be a disappointment, and it is for these countries that we must take the necessary precautions so that they can participate at a later stage, say, by the year 2001.

QUESTION: And what will happen with those countries that persistently do not want to participate?

MR. WALTER: I just do not think it will work for countries to pursue their own discretionary exchange rate policy over the long term and expect at the same time to remain unlimited partners in a single internal market. We must at least guarantee that these countries cannot make use of exchange rates to create an unfair competitive advantage. It simply is not right for a country to act in an isolationist manner, on the one hand, doing whatever it wants without consideration for its partners, and, on the other, expect its partners to deal with it like every other fully integrated partner. This remains an important issue for which we still have no answer.

QUESTION: What will determine the stability of the future currency?

MR. WALTER: First and foremost, the policy of the European Central Bank, an institution we do not yet really know because it does not exist. What we do know is what the law says about it, and the law governing the European Central Bank is the stability-oriented law of any central bank: a clear, well-defined goal of price stability and a great deal of independence from everyday influences. I have a theory that when the European Central Bank takes off, the market will still not believe that it is as good as, say, the Bundesbank. But I also reckon that the market will see that, when faced with doubts about stability, the European Central Bank will behave in exactly the same way as the Deutsche Bundesbank has always behaved when faced with the same circumstances. That is to say, it will react forcefully to secure stability. And it is then that the European Central Bank will come to win the trust of the market very quickly.

QUESTION: And what will become of the Bundesbank?

MR. WALTER: The Bundesbank is one of the national banks that will be dealing with the central bank in this European system. That is to say, the president of the Bundesbank will automatically be a governor of the European Central Bank. To put it more clearly, the Bundesbank will be a branch of the European Central Bank. The former will then no longer make monetary policy independently but will execute the policy arrived at by the European Central Bank.

QUESTION: Federal Minister of Finance Waigel has called for a "stability pact" among countries. Is this an adequate measure to secure stability? Or would you propose something else?

MR. WALTER: The Maastricht Treaty basically calls for financial discipline. Those who do not adhere to such a discipline can face sanctions, a measure that would, however, require a decision by the Council of Ministers. Minister Waigel's proposal calls for these sanctions to take effect automatically. I think that is a sensible path to take, and many governments agree. Furthermore, I do have my own ideas on this subject. I harbor a certain sympathy for the idea of writing the Maastricht regulations into national constitutions. Another possibility would be to make use of rating agencies, such as exist in the United States, which would assess the financial policies of individual regional authorities. Those that perform less well would be hit with an interest surcharge, while the sounder debtors would pay lower interest, just as credit ratings are assessed in business.

QUESTION: A single currency will mean equality of wages and salaries but will not affect what a person actually takes home. In the last analysis, will there not have to be a reconciliation in tax systems?

MR. WALTER: Currency union is neither currency reform nor social reform. In the United States, for example, which has had a single currency for more than a century, wage differences between Nebraska and New York are similar to differences in Europe between Portugal and the wealthiest countries. Comparability does not have to mean equality.

There should be discrepancies in direct taxation if a particular state offers different services. Such differences will bring about competition in tax rates. But what is not good are differences in indirect taxes, such as a one-mark mineral oil tax on a liter of gasoline in one place and just half that in another.

QUESTION: Even though citizens are anxious about the stability of the currency, this currency union is designed finally to bring about political stability in Europe. To this end, which prerequisites will be met?

MR. WALTER: The Maastricht Treaty is excellent in regard to technical issues relating to currency union. On other points, however, it provides only provisional answers, and the signatories know that. And this is why the Maastricht Treaty stipulates the 1996 Intergovernmental Conference. That will be the opportunity to make improvements in the lack of progress toward political union. Whoever wants a single market and no more borders cannot continue to pursue national policies. A national immigration policy with open borders does not work any more. And whoever wishes to form a common immigration policy can no longer make different foreign policies; the same goes for defense policies. This is our homework for 1996–1997.

QUESTION: While the discussion about currency reform is picking up speed in Europe, we hear almost nothing from Japan or the United States. How interested are these two economic powers in this process?

MR. WALTER: The Japanese are following this process closely and with some admiration. They even envy us because, unlike Europeans, they do not have any close friends in their neighborhood. The Americans have always viewed Europe soberly. In official circles, the currency union is being looked on with goodwill.

PART TWO
Political Cooperation

Introduction to Part Two

As Europe experiences its growing pains, Atlanticism is also being rethought. Questions about burden sharing and American leadership arise once again. Absent the sturdy framework of cold war discipline, the North Atlantic Treaty Organization is challenged to redefine its mission, to admit new members, and to address new threats. In Europe, attempts to forge a Common Foreign and Security Policy have foundered but not disappeared. The campaign for European unity—for monetary and political union—remains on track. It is fraught, however, with conflict and contradiction. British Euro-skeptics and German federalists remain deeply divided. Countries such as Denmark and Sweden worry about sovereignty issues raised by potential membership in a monetary union. Questions about the European Union's growing democracy deficit remain unanswered. What would it mean for the United States if a Common Foreign and Security Policy were adopted and CFSP paralyzed the policies of countries that have been important partners for the United States? What would it mean for Europe if nothing meaningful came into place? How will issues of democracy and sovereignty be resolved? What are the consequences if the campaign designed to bring Europe closer together does not succeed?

Further European Integration Is Inevitable

Stanimir A. Alexandrov

Foreign counsel, Powell, Goldstein, Frazer & Murphy

The forces of gravity in Europe prevail over the centrifugal forces. Thus, not only are the enlargement of the European Union and the unification of Europe desirable, but also they are inevitable.

After the end of the cold war, two seemingly contradictory trends have dominated in Europe. On the one hand, there has been a trend toward integration in Western Europe. The Maastricht Treaty created the European Union with three pillars: the European Community, the Common Foreign and Security Policy, and the Justice and Home Affairs Cooperation. The creation of the European Union was a major step toward further economic and political integration. The Intergovernmental Conference of the European Union, which started in Turin in March 1996 and is expected to produce its results sometime in 1997, has the major task of promoting European values and democracy, making the European Union more relevant to its citizens, and enabling the union to work better in preparing for enlargement. Enhancing the democratic representation in the union, not only of member states but also of their peoples, is an important tool in achieving this goal. It includes increasing the role of the European Parliament and improving the decision-making process of the council. Eliminating the so-called democratic deficit would be one of the major achievements of the conference.

On the other hand, the eastern part of the European continent has tended toward disintegration. The former Soviet Union broke apart. Russia, itself a federation, has been resisting secessionist pressures and has not shied away from using force to do so. Czechoslovakia split peacefully; the former Yugoslavia disintegrated, in part peacefully and in part through the bloodiest conflict in Europe since World War II. National and ethnic tensions in parts of Eastern Europe and the former Soviet Union are a major threat to peace and stability.

Trend toward Integration

These two trends are only seemingly contradictory. The long-term trend is clearly toward integration. As of January 1, 1995, the European Union expanded from twelve members to fifteen, its fourth enlargement. Twelve other countries are associated with the European Union: Cyprus and Malta, six Central and Eastern European countries (Bulgaria, the Czech Republic, Hungary, Poland, Romania, and Slovakia), the three Baltic countries, and one of the former Yugoslav republics (Slovenia). Other former Yugoslav and Soviet republics will eventually seek associated status. All twelve associated countries aspire to full membership. Each one of them insists on acceding to the European Union as soon as possible. The Central and Eastern European countries have created their own free trade area—the Central European Free Trade Area—which is seen as a vehicle for speedier accession to the European Union.

Association, in addition to substantial opening of markets (phased elimination of tariffs and increased market access), allows active involvement in the common foreign and security policy and in the justice and home affairs cooperation. The associated countries, while eager to participate in the discussion on the future of European integration, realize that they will become part of whatever the European Union is at the time of their accession. These countries have expressed little concern about losing their cultural identity, national heritage, or national identity; their major concern has been to improve the efficiency and the competitiveness of their economies and their standard of living.

Objectives of Integration

Still the question remains, What should be the objectives of European integration? In economic terms, the goals have been set: the creation of the EU internal market and the European Monetary Union. In political terms, the situation is less clear, and the views expressed have been more controversial. Integration in the broadest sense may be an impossible task: to create a European identity, while preserving the national and ethnic identities of the constituent parts of the union. Nevertheless, the European Union seems to have taken this road: the Maastricht Treaty has set the goal of creating a citizenship of the union in addition to, and not instead of, national citizenship. The treaty sets forth specific rights of the union's citizens. The Intergovernmental Conference is considering expanding those rights. Will this effort ignite a more vigorous conflict between the European identity and the national identity?

European and National Identity

The assumption that the European and the national identities are in conflict is wrong. National and ethnic communities in Europe strive to espouse the European values and become involved in European integration. With the enlargement of the European Union and the progress of integration, the nation-state will inevitably become more of an intermediary between pan-European and regional interests. The nation-state will, of course, remain a symbol of national culture, pride, and identity, the guarantor of the preservation of the national heritage. But in practical terms, the traditional paradigm of local versus national will be transformed into local versus European.

It is easier to identify and analyze this trend in the multiethnic European countries (separatist movements are not uncharacteristic of Western Europe, either). Why, for example, would the two communities in Belgium prefer their federal state to a federal European organization? The Basques in Spain? The separatists in northern Italy? The unionists and the republicans in Northern Ireland? Would not national, ethnic, or religious minorities feel more comfortable under the common umbrella of a European federal organization than they do now? Would the Hungarian minority in Romania, for example, prefer an isolated Romanian nation-state to a Romania integrated into a pan-European structure? Why is part of the solution in Bosnia a loose federation with the participation of the Bosnian Serbs and the Bosnian Croats?

There are examples of successful unions. One of the "success stories" in the modern world is the United States of America, a voluntary union of formerly independent states. The U.S. example illustrates two very important points: (1) to succeed, the unification process has to develop through democratic and transparent procedures, something the EU Intergovernmental Conference should pay special attention to; and (2) it takes a bold and broad vision to initiate the process of unification and many years to mold it to the imperatives of reality.

We sometimes forget about those success stories of unification. Americans remain skeptical about the process of integration in Europe. In the fall of 1995, an article in the *Washington Post* described the Court of Justice of the European Community as an "obscure court," which claims jurisdiction over sovereign states. Few Americans seem to make an adequate analogy with the Supreme Court of the United States. From a European perspective, it may seem equally strange that Americans have placed their states and their Union in the hands of nine Supreme Court justices who have the final say on a tremendous number of important matters relating to the U.S. Constitution, federal and state law, public order, social structure, culture, economy, and human rights.

What makes the example of the United States different is that the states of the United States did not, and do not, possess the distinct cultural identity and national heritage in which European countries take such pride. Yet states in Europe have been willing to delegate to the union, at least in part, their powers in a number of areas: in trade and investment, macroeconomic regulation, human and workers' rights, and large areas of lawmaking and to a lesser extent in foreign policy, defense, and "internal" security. In many of those and other areas, the governments of nation-states may be reduced to the role currently reserved for local and regional governments. The distinct cultural heritage, however, will contribute to preserving national identities, so that the nation-state will retain its role as a symbol and a guardian of this heritage.

Political and Military Integration

It may now seem difficult to translate this idea of unification into the specific terms of political and military integration. Yet we have witnessed impressive achievements in trade and economic relations. What began as a free trade area and later a customs union is now an economic union with common policies that may soon be expanded to a monetary union. In addition, free trade arrangements proliferate. The enlargement of the European Union will expand the free trade area in Europe. The union has engaged in liberalizing trade with Russia, Ukraine, and other European countries, as well as with the non-European countries of the Mediterranean. The customs union between the European Union and Turkey has already been approved. Trade discussions have been initiated with the MERCOSUR countries. Trade arrangements between the United States and the European Union will affect the North American Free Trade Agreement. All those arrangements liberalizing trade will eventually have an effect on the whole structure of the General Agreement on Tariffs and Trade and the World Trade Organization. Are we really very far away from a "worldwide" free trade zone?

The changes in trade and economic relations since 1957, when the Treaty of Rome was signed, have been extensive. It was as difficult to anticipate them then as it is to anticipate now the progress of political and military integration in five or ten years.

The Maastricht Treaty already refers to a common defense policy, "which might in time lead to a common defense." The Western European Union aspires to play an active role in peacekeeping and in European defense. Discussions are taking place in NATO to allow the organization's European members to take military measures without the direct involvement and participation of the United States. Contemporary threats to security include such unconventional security risks as terrorism, nuclear proliferation, and the (alas, already) typical post–cold war conflicts: ethnic, national, and religious. Dealing with those security threats requires a new level of political and military integration, a new type of common foreign and security policy, and enhanced cooperation in justice and home affairs. If the European Union is to pursue those goals effectively, it needs to create the necessary institutional structures.

Enlarging and Deepening the Union

This need is more obvious in view of the enlargement of the union. A union of twenty-seven or more countries could hardly achieve any kind of foreign policy, defense, and security cooperation without taking further steps to deepen its political integration. The discussion of the advantages of enlargement as opposed to the advantages of deepening the process of integration is moot in that it considers enlargement and further integration as alternatives. In reality, there is no alternative to enlargement as there is no alternative to deepening the integration within the European Union.

A consensus has emerged on the necessity and inevitability of enlargement both in the current member states of the European Union and, remarkably, among the various political forces in the countries aspiring to membership. The question is how soon the candidates will be ready for membership and what arrangements should be made to speed up the transition process.

The assumption is that economic, not political or security, considerations will play the decisive role in determining the terms and the timing of the associated countries' full membership. This proposition reflects the understanding that political integration does not stand in the way of enlargement. The associated countries of Central and Eastern Europe are willing to be part of the process of political and economic integration and to share the values espoused by the European Union and its member-states. The major question is the extent to which those countries are ready to bear the pressures of the internal market of the union. Yet to wait until their economies are on par with the economies of the current EU members would be a mistake: this may not happen unless they join the union, and has certainly not been the case when other applicants, current EU members, were admitted. The associated countries should become full participants in the political and economic integration of the European Union to transform their economies faster, become competitive, and improve their standard of living.

Although it is apparently too early to speak of a federal state of Europe, the only way to achieve the goals of the European Union—peace and prosperity—is further political and economic integration. This process will be long and perhaps sometimes painful, touched by controversy and debate. Yet it is unthinkable that this process should stop.

Common Heritage, Constructive Rivalry

Dennis L. Bark
Senior fellow, Hoover Institution

Will the ties between Europe and the United States, forged during forty years of the cold war, atrophy? The answer is in two parts. First, how strong are the ties that bind together the new continent and the old? Second, will the Europeans, will the Americans, provide strong leadership? Or will they continue to drift, as they have been doing since 1990?

To be sure, during the cold war the existence of a common adversary—dictatorship in Central and Eastern Europe and in the former Soviet Union—produced a common defense alliance. There were some good reasons for doing so. The threat to freedom in Europe was easy to see, in the form of the Warsaw Pact. The missiles pointed toward Western Europe provided a powerful incentive to join forces in the form of the North Atlantic Treaty Organization. As long as the threat continued, there was every reason to maintain that alliance, and that is exactly what happened. What was less clear, however, was what would happen if the threat disappeared. Would the ties unravel that bound Europeans and Americans together in NATO? Or would a common heritage, shared values, and shared interests be strong enough to bind Europe and America together in the future as well?

In 1997, in the absence of a clear threat to freedom in Europe posed by Communist dictatorship, it is logical to ask what the ties are made of and how strong they are. The answer is straightforward enough. The ties that bind both continents are based on common values. They are based on a history of shared interests, forged not during 40 years, but during 376 years, since the Pilgrims landed at Plymouth Rock, and among the Europeans many centuries before that. The relationship thrives because it embraces what unites, not what divides. It is based on a social, economic, political, and cultural heritage that Europe and the United States have in common. It is based on a common interest in peace and freedom, as well as on a political commitment to the principles of liberty and justice. It is based on the mutually shared political will to honor these values.

Today, our knowledge of our common heritage is very much with us. We also continue to share, as Europeans and Americans, common interests in ensuring the viability and security of what may properly be called our Atlantic civilization. But as history teaches us, the decline, collapse, and implosion of an empire—in this case, the Soviet Empire—brings with it long-term consequences. We will be interpreting and responding to these consequences for decades. Indeed, a great Communist empire still exists, called China. It will undoubtedly prove to be an object of economic rivalry between Europe and America, but China also represents a political challenge we share. What kind of balance vis-à-vis the last great Communist empire do we, as transatlantic partners, want to strike between containment and détente? A common heritage, common interests, and an alliance created for a threat that no longer exists are not enough to meet the new challenges facing Europe and America. We must, very soon, find new answers for new challenges that affect both continents.

For example, there are challenges to our security interests. Direct and indirect threats to freedom continue to exist, both within and without Europe, including dictatorships large and small, which either singly or in combination have the potential to do serious damage to the peace and prosperity of the transatlantic world. The threats are also specific in nature, such as ethnic and religious hatred, drug traffic, environmental degradation, criminal business enterprises that challenge legitimate governments, nuclear proliferation, the activities of rogue states like Libya, Iraq, or North Korea, and terrorism. Finally, thoughtful Europeans and Americans alike are asking themselves how to compete effectively in rapidly expanding markets of international trade. The European Union, with a population of more than 370 million, can become one of the world's most important economic regions, along with the Association of South East Asian Nations region of more than 320 million people and the North America Free Trade Area of 360 million people. Similar challenges can be seen in the new investment and financial markets in Europe and in Asia.

Both Europe and America have a continuing interest in meeting threats well before they reach our own respective borders, as well as in promoting prosperity and working for peace around the globe. To do so successfully in today's world, Europe and America must ensure that their partnership reflects a balanced division of labor. Moreover, the Europeans as a whole must develop the cohesive political will to make credible their commitment to transatlantic responsibilities. Enormous power is contained in the ties that unite Europe and America, in the common heritage created over almost four centuries. So, how do we use that power effectively?

What Needs to Be Done?

Let us recall that freedom won the cold war. The reconstruction of Europe, the defense of Berlin, the preservation of peace in postwar Europe, the fall of the Berlin Wall, the collapse of Communist dictatorship, the unification of Germany, and the collapse of the Soviet Union were not accidents. They were the result of a competitive process between freedom and suppression.

Democracy prevailed because of communism's corruption and injustice, and because the Europeans and Americans summoned the political will to contain it. They formed a constructive partnership between Western Europe and the United States, which could just as easily be called a constructive rivalry. They did not always see things the same way and did not always agree. But their rivalry, when it did emerge, produced better debate and wiser decisions. Because Europeans and Americans often brought from their two continents different perspectives to bear on the same issue, it made their partnership stronger.

There are some excellent examples:

- Willy Brandt's *Ostpolitik* was widely criticized in the United States and in some European countries as well, but it nonetheless played a constructive role on the path toward German unity and toward the collapse of communism.
- Although disagreements existed between Helmut Schmidt and Jimmy Carter, Schmidt's support for NATO's double-track decision was instrumental in setting the stage for the dramatic changes in Europe during the 1980s.
- European support for the Conference on Security and Cooperation in Europe during the 1970s was strong and was maligned in the United States; but in the aftermath of the Velvet Revolution of 1989, it became clear that the Europeans had been right—the CSCE had been an invaluable tool for those opposing their respective communist dictatorships in Central and Eastern Europe.
- In 1990 the two-plus-four talks that led to the unification of Germany reflected both constructive partnership and constructive rivalry among Americans, English, French, and Germans, with the result that united Germany, like West Germany in the past, would have the opportunity to play a major role in shaping the future transatlantic partnership. Since 1990, however, not everything has gone smoothly.

NATO's Future

Take, first, the case of NATO. Is the alliance equal to the new challenges presented by a continent no longer divided into two military blocs? The task is the same: to preserve peace. The problems, however, are different. They are found in *how* NATO's members define its purpose in a dramatically changed European world. Thus far, the definition is lacking. As Yugoslavia began to disintegrate, NATO's European members said they would solve the problem. When they could not agree, they justified their failure to act by explaining they could not agree. Thereafter, they asserted that what had become a full-fledged war was a United Nations problem. It then became, as a consequence of a highly confusing series of events, a NATO problem, as well as a UN problem, and finally also a U.S. problem. Whose responsibility is it?

The point is clear: NATO's members, and particularly the Europeans, have to decide whether protecting the national security of its members includes keeping peace in Europe. They have to decide what their security interests are. Does the alliance want to develop a new policy of containment, to intervene in smaller conflicts on the periphery of the crumbling Soviet Empire, or in the Middle East? What role does this decision assign to the United States? Does America wish to become involved in local conflicts in Europe indefinitely, or are the Europeans obligated, able, and willing to assume the responsibility? What, in these considerations, is the role of united Germany? Is Germany willing to commit troops to deal with conflicts elsewhere, both in Europe and abroad? Whatever the shape of NATO in the future, Germany's position in it is crucial to NATO's success or failure as a credible alliance. Germany must take a leading role in defining the purpose of the alliance.

Until the latter is accomplished, any discussion about expanding NATO as an alliance without a purpose is putting the cart before the horse. Indeed, seen from the perspective of those making concerted efforts to support the democratic process in Russia, with whom NATO seeks no quarrel, there is every reason to proceed consistently and systematically. In the words of Vladimir Lukin, the chairman of the Duma Foreign Relations Committee and an ally of the liberal opposition leader Grigory Yavlinsky:

> If NATO wants to expand to Eastern Europe, then first there must be a long process of international discussion, involving Russia, about what NATO is, and what the threats to security in the region really are and how they can be countered. . . . Russian policy . . . remains to try to influence NATO by cooperating with it—hence the decision to join the Partnership for Peace. An additional reason for this policy is that although the anger of Russian diplomats over NATO behavior is unfeigned, more serious and less paranoid Russians do of course realize that NATO represents no threat of direct attack on Russia. Indeed, the Western alliance's display of weakness, cowardice, and internal divisions over Bosnia has diminished Russian fears of NATO as an organization.[1]

1. Anatol Lieven, "A New Iron Curtain," *Atlantic Monthly*, January 1996, pp. 20–25.

The European Union's Future

Take, second, the European Community. The fifteen members of the European Union have created a single market, without tariffs and without borders. But the EU is not a union of European countries; it is a union of selected European countries. Thus, it is easy to understand why the new democratic governments of Poland, Hungary, or the Czech Republic, for example, resent the refusal of the EU to admit them as members and why they find it enormously frustrating that the EU has placed tariffs on a whole host of goods from the latter countries. There are, without doubt, strong arguments why it would be a major economic mistake to allow the weak economies of the countries of Central Europe equal status with the current members of the EU. But are punitive tariffs in anyone's interest, if we want those economies to become stronger?

The members of the European Union, the majority of whom are also members of NATO, must decide what kind of economic community they want to have. Should economic union include all European countries? Is the European Union going to become a bureaucratic monster living in Brussels? It seems clear, at least to many Americans who are seeking to give form and substance to a new transatlantic partnership, that an economic European union makes a great deal of sense. Economic competition based on free markets enriches trade and produces better products at lower prices for a greater number of people than does any other form of commerce.

The idea of political community, however, appears much more vague. The members of the EU seem to be betraying their own political ideals, in that the EU has always claimed it is more than just an economic community. But in former Yugoslavia they could not summon the political will to act together, so they failed to assume responsibility for what they insisted was a European problem requiring European solution. Until the Europeans can give the phrase *political will* constructive meaning, any movement to create new European political institutions would be a major mistake. Continued absence of cohesive political will is going to make it increasingly difficult to define the transatlantic partnership of the future. This is an unacceptable condition for both Europe and America. Further integration in Europe is, on the contrary, in the interests of both Europe and America, as two scholars of European affairs, one from Germany and one from the United States, point out:

It is obviously in the best interests of both Europe and America not to relinquish the innovation of European integration, and to continue to pursue and support further moves toward the political unification of Europe. . . . [however,] the stepwise restructuring of transatlantic relations on the lines of a symmetrical and balanced alliance (coupled with greater cooperation with Russia) is not inevitable, and there are alternatives. But it is a realistic vision capable of realization. And it provides an opportunity to combine continuity and change in the Euro-Atlantic area in a constructive manner.[2]

The end of the cold war has created the problem of how to make constructive rivalry work as effectively in the future as it did for more than forty years, from 1949 to 1990. It would be wise, as we consider how to solve it, to recall that this is a problem of success, not of failure. Europe is free for the first time in more than half a century. Common heritage and constructive rivalry played a decisive role in the postwar history of the transatlantic partnership, culminating in the events of 1989–1990. Both can do so again; but central to the whole proposition of partnership is the quality of leadership in European capitals as well as in Washington, D.C.

If there exists what some scholars and politicians call the imperative of American leadership, there also exists, in my view, the imperative of European leadership. Together, they equal partnership. Knowledge of history sent this message to Europeans and Americans in the wake of World War II, and the result was transatlantic partnership. Indeed, one of Europe's greatest leaders recognized the importance of the past in 1946, as a basis on which to build the future:

Knowledge of the past is the only foundation we have from which to peer into and try to measure the future. Expert knowledge, however indispensable, is no substitute for a generous and comprehending outlook upon the human story with all its sadness and with all its unquenchable hope.[3]

---

2. Miles Kahler and Werner Link, *Europe and America* (New York: Council on Foreign Relations Press, 1996), pp. 105–107.
3. Winston Churchill, University of Miami, February 1946.

Knowledge of the past is indispensable, if we know where we are going. What knowledge of the past does not tell us is how much time Europe and America have left to design, once again, a trans atlantic partnership based on common heritage and constructive rivalry.

A Reply to Václav Klaus and Other Euro-Skeptics

CHRISTOPH BERTRAM
Diplomatic correspondent, Die Zeit

Czech Prime Minister Václav Klaus has often been a man of vision. But when he and others talk about integration in the European Union, they are wearing blinders. And when he promises a velvet revolution in Brussels, referring to the overthrow of the Communist regime in his own country, he is not only making a preposterous comparison to the dedicated parliamentarians, officials, and politicians involved in the decision making of the European Union but also revealing an amazing lack of perception of how Europe works—and making his country less welcome in what is and will remain a central pillar of European prosperity and order.

Misunderstandings about Integration

That attitude would not be especially worrying if these were merely the views of someone who, through no fault of his own, had been kept out of European integration by decades of Soviet control; people of Klaus's intelligence are usually quick studies. It is worrying because his statements echo those held by an increasingly vociferous group of people who always had the chance to know better and once did know better, particularly if not exclusively in the Anglo-Saxon world. In Britain, the Conservative Party has been tearing itself to pieces over Europe, often for purely tactical considerations of intraparty rivalries but also because, as Britain's international role has become marginalized, of a deep resentment against a European Union that seems to have moved to center stage. In the United States, which under both Republican and Democratic administrations was decisive for the initial breakthroughs of European integration in the 1950s, the old conviction that peace among European nations requires a pooling of their national sovereignties seems to have given way either to angry impatience with the slow progress of European integration or to smug condescension, more a product of a current mood of overconfidence than of serious analysis.

According to these views, aspirations for European political union are poppycock if not outright dangerous, and European integration is and should be about no more than free trade in a free market. But this notion reveals two fundamental misunderstandings: first, European integration has always been about political union even when disguised as economic integration; and second, economic integration by itself, without the underpinning of political integration, will not last.

From the beginning, political integration among member states has been the end and economic cooperation the means for those working for a united Europe. This relationship was perhaps more evident to the generation emerging from World War II than to that emerging from the cold war. The lesson that most continental European countries learned from World War II was that the traditional way of doing business among governments, with the bigger countries doing what they want and the smaller suffering what they must, was the recipe for the disaster that lay behind them. They realized the need to develop new ways of interaction, based not on brute power but on equality in common institutions—with equality no longer pursued, as in the past, through the competing claim of national sovereignty but through the creative involvement in mechanisms of common decision making in which individual nation-states, whatever their weight, no longer wield veto power.

When in May 1950 the foreign minister of France, Robert Schuman, issued an invitation to establish common institutions for the sectors of coal and steel, seen at the time as essential ingredients of national power, the Netherlands, Belgium, Luxembourg, Italy, and West Germany responded enthusiastically. The Coal and Steel Community opened for business under the presidency of Jean Monnet, the architect of the Schuman Plan, in August 1952. It was the decisive first step, the breakthrough out of Europe's conflict-generating past.

The novelty of the undertaking is that for the first time, sovereign countries agreed to subject matters hitherto under their exclusive jurisdiction to institutions not fully under their control. As the forerunner of a European constitution, the Schuman Plan curbed the monopoly of national governments through common procedures and a separation of powers in a new community, between an executive (the high authority, later the commission), a legislative assembly (the Council of Ministers plus an embryonic parliamentary body, now the European Parliament), and the European Court of Justice.

What was established for coal and steel was extended a few years later to a common market. But for the countries participating in it—the six founders were progressively joined by practically all West European countries so that the total stands at fifteen today—the central aspect was that, with each further step of pooling national sovereignties, they would move closer to an inseparable, comprehensive political community. The Maastricht Treaty of 1991 formally established the European Union. It was ratified by all members, including Tory-ruled Britain, and now forms the basis for all future admissions. The primacy of the political objective is not merely implied but made doubly explicit: through committing member states to "an ever closer union" and through laying the groundwork for a European currency and a European central bank by 1999 as well as including both foreign policy and defense among the union's ultimate tasks.

Political Purpose

Given the history of integration and the text of treaties duly signed and ratified, there can be no doubt whatsoever about the political purpose of the European exercise. It is true, of course, that questions about how close-knit this community of states will ultimately be remain; nothing can be less surprising than that member states themselves are not quite sure and not quite in agreement over where the balance between the prerogatives of the nation-state and the jurisdiction of the union will lie. But to juxtapose, as Václav Klaus does (along with many others), a "Europe of nation-states" to a "federal Europe" smacks of an attempt to turn back the degree of integration already achieved under the guise of false alternatives. The nature of the new European community lies precisely in the combination of both.

The nation-state will persist; yet its evident interdependence with others will be conducted in common institutions expressing the common interest. The balance between the elements is dynamic, with some countries determined to go further in the direction of common decision making than others. But it is not a matter of either-or, not even of opposing ideologies. Rather, it is a matter of judgment about how much more needs to be integrated to keep the common effort from sliding back and what measures should be taken to prepare the union for what must be its next major strategic task, namely the admission of East European democracies into its midst.

Maintaining the momentum of integration to prevent regression requires a degree of political cohesion. Free trade and a free market are, no doubt, in the interest of all Europe's citizens. But a free market is by definition competitive: success means profit for one and loss for another, jobs for some and unemployment for others. Competition is likely to generate resentment against the most powerful economic player, constantly raising the danger of a relapse into protectionism by the weaker ones as well as producing political misgivings and tensions. Europe, after all, experienced something like a free market before World War I; in the absence of political institutions capable of transcending the nation-state, the slide into conflict was unchecked. A free trade area without an overarching political purpose expressing a common good that constrains economic discrepancies among the members will, therefore, not last. If such a Europe is what Václav Klaus has in mind, he had better think again.

He also better think again about the consequences his velvet revolution would have on the ability of the European Union to take in new members, the Czech Republic included. The EU's institutions, which were designed for its six founding members, are already clogging up under the present membership of fifteen countries, each keen to make its influence felt and determined to block decisions it judges contrary to its interests. The result has been a growing inefficiency of EU institutions and a gradual renationalization of decision making. Unless the efficiency of EU actions is considerably improved, taking in new members would mean a gridlocked union, scarcely an attractive body to join.

This is the dilemma of "deepening" and "widening." Without greater willingness of today's members to grant greater powers to the common institutions and reduce the ability of national governments to block decisions by veto, the EU will not be able to do what is now imperative for European stability—to invite the new democracies of Eastern Europe into its midst. Unfortunately, that willingness cannot be assumed for all the union's present members, some of whom even see enlargement not at all as a reason for strengthening supranational structures but as a chance to weaken them. This view makes it unlikely that the union will be fit for enlargement. Yet the pressure to admit at least some new members from what used to be Soviet-controlled Eastern Europe will prove irresistible. Instead of deepening before widening, the union will find itself in the awkward position of extending its membership with weak institutions that can only be weakened further in the process. If all those now queuing at the EU's door are let in within the next decade, membership will roughly double, and the union will become little more than an intergovernmental agency for free trade and free markets. For the reasons put forward above, this will be tantamount to the collapse of European integration. The union will lose its ability to promote both prosperity for its members and stability for all of Europe.

Some EU members at least are determined to prevent such a development. That group, clustered around the states that founded the European Community back in the 1950s, is now arguing for an avant-garde within the widening union that, since not all members are willing to push ahead with integration, will organize closer cooperation among those who are, while inviting others to join them when they are ready. The model for such an inner core has already been agreed on in the Maastricht Treaty: European monetary union implies, for the limited group of members likely to qualify, the introduction of a common currency under the authority of an independent European central bank. The advent of monetary union, almost certain to take place on January 1, 1999, the date laid down in the treaty, will create a union within the EU, probably not just limiting itself to monetary matters but extending cooperation among participants into other areas as well.

Monetary union thus has become the best hope for those who fear that the trend of renationalization coupled with enlargement will mean the end of European integration. That danger is real, and perhaps even the Václav Klauses in Europe may come to recognize it someday, ideally before it is too late. For centuries, European thinkers have dreamed of a united Europe. That dream was given its first serious chance of realization when the devastation of war had exposed the bankruptcy of the old European state system and when American leadership provided the security assurance necessary to encourage European nations to trust their fate instead to common institutions. The European Union, in all its imperfections but also with all its potential, is the result of this extraordinary historical window of opportunity.

Those who call today for a Europe of nation-states rather than a federal Europe have either forgotten that history or do not understand it. If the window should close again as a result of the egotism of states and the shortsightedness of their leaders, all of Europe will suffer, not least Eastern and Central Europe, which have already suffered so much.

Nationalism and the Superstate

BILL CASH
Member of Parliament (Britain)

A specter haunts the chancelleries of Europe, and none more so than the chancellery of Germany: the specter of nationalism. Unlike the specter of revolution in mid-nineteenth-century Europe, this one exists only in politicians' minds. Not that nationalism is dead. On the contrary, despite the assertions of the architects of the European Union, national feelings remain the most powerful force in modern politics. But Chancellor Kohl, President Chirac, and others confuse two totally different phenomena: nationalism and the modern democratic national state.

Realities of Nationalism

The European project grew out of the devastations of the Second World War, which was erroneously perceived to have been caused by rampant nationalism. In fact, Nazism, just like its counterpart in the East, communism, was a supranational ideology that sought to unite Europe in the name of a certain vision of a corporate, regulated society. Though expansionist in Europe, it was inward looking as far as the rest of the world was concerned. Many of its economic ideas were not dissimilar from the more recent ones of monetary union, an exchange-rate mechanism, an independent central bank situated in Germany, and so on. Whether the national or the socialist part of National Socialism was more important, Hitler's Germany could not be called a modern democratic national state.

In the devastated Europe of 1945, it was easy to assume that the way to prevent another war on that scale was to work toward the integration and eventual unification of the different national states, to overcome the national feelings that had apparently caused a great tragedy. Not only did this analysis misunderstand the nature of Nazism and of nationalism, it misread the new military and strategic problems. With the advent of the nuclear age and the development of the cold war, the focus shifted further east in Europe, toward the Soviet Union and its forcibly subsumed satellites. Germany was still at the center of the problem but in a different way. It was no longer the potential aggressor but a symbol of a divided Europe and the possible weak link in the alliance against the Soviet Union.

It is easy to forget that throughout the nineteenth century nationalism was perceived as a progressive, liberal cause. The fight for national self-determination was waged against what was seen as a number of oppressive, obscurantist regimes. Britain, as the foremost democratic state in Europe, supported the fight. The reasons were not entirely altruistic. For centuries, the cardinal tenet of English, then British, foreign policy was to prevent the formation of a united European state, whether under Spanish or French rulers. The national movements of Europe would undermine all such attempts. It was further assumed that the newly formed national states would be, in the main, liberal in politics and democratic in constitution. As such, they would be likely allied with Britain. It was obvious then, and ought to be now, that democratic states do not wage war against each other.

Another aspect of the nineteenth century drive toward national self-determination was the push toward the creation of larger states, though some factors served to undermine the multinational empires, such as the Austro-Hungarian and the Russian. The most obvious examples are Italy and Germany. In both cases, a number of small states with the same language and the same culture felt themselves to be part of the same nation and sought to form a unified state to express all this politically. One cannot, however, assume that the unification of these is in any way similar to the creation of the European Union, any more than one can assume that the United States of Europe is an entity that in any way resembles the United States of America. In all these cases, political union expressed the cultural, linguistic, and, to some extent, national union that had preceded it. In the case of the European Union, nothing of that kind exists. The political union is preceding everything else. The nearest comparison to that in the modern world is the artificially created USSR.

In the case of Germany, the creation of a modern state has been a painful process. The first German Empire was forged in a succession of wars. Bismarck, the architect of the new Germany—which was different from that dreamt of by the liberal nationalists of the 1840s and 1850s—refrained from any other hostility after 1871. Other German politicians and, above all, Emperor William II had other ideas. There is no space here to go into the debates about the causes of the First World War, and, truth to tell, no European country was blameless. Suffice it to say that the war dealt a devastating blow to European politics and European hegemony. From the chaos that followed the four years of fighting and the collapse of the various empires, from the revolutions, counterrevolutions, terror, and counterterror, a new and potentially equally harmful idea emerged: the need to overcome nationalism. From the beginning, this idea confused the sort of national militarism that had held sway in Imperial Germany with democratic nationalism. Nevertheless, the idea was reinforced by the experience of the Second World War. Many early architects of the European Union misunderstood the Soviet Union. They saw only its strength, not the underlying contradictions. They saw coherence and planning and often refused to see that these were achieved by terror.

Postwar Europe and Later

Throughout the 1950s and 1960s and, even, the 1970s, as Western Europe recovered from the ordeal, as newly democratized countries became eligible to join the European Economic Community, there appeared to be some economic sense to the project. Though "ever closer union" had been laid down in the Treaty of Rome of 1957, political unification was apparently postponed, though not forgotten, in favor of economic development. Throughout these years, Western Europe was protected by the North Atlantic Treaty Organization, the American military presence, and the nuclear umbrella. Eastern Europe did not fare quite so well. Economically backward because of an imposed ideology, its national feelings artificially suppressed, that whole area seethed under the surface to explode periodically: in 1953 in East Germany, in 1956 in Hungary, in 1968 in Czechoslovakia, in 1980 in Poland. Within the Soviet Union itself, nationalist organizations formed and consolidated.

In the 1980s, the situation began to change. Economically, Western Europe began to stagnate. The reasons are not hard to find. The now rapidly developing drive toward political unification was creating unfavorable economic conditions through excessive centralization, regulation, and harmonization. The undoubted benefits of the single market were undermined because it was based on the idea of harmonization rather than mutual product recognition. The latter would have kept the single market as an economic entity, a highly beneficial free market. But the aim was a political union, one that was, furthermore, based on a semisocialist, wholly corporatist, planned model. Harmonization, which is inimical to free trade, was essential to it.

At the same time, the Communist world began to change. For whatever reason, the East European countries were allowed to break away from their big brother, and they joyously embraced the ideas of political and economic freedom as well as those of nationalism. For them, nationalism had been a factor in the fight against political oppression and economic stagnation. The collapse of the Soviet Union, swiftly followed, and with even more bloodshed, by that of Yugoslavia, showed the folly and danger of forcibly created federal states. But what upset the equation in the West was the reunification of Germany. The new German state was, by far, the largest and most powerful within the European Union. At least one purpose of the European project had been to control Germany. From 1989, it looked increasingly as if, on the contrary, Germany would control the union. Curiously enough, the people who were most frightened by that idea were the Germans themselves.

The arguments about monetary union have long gone beyond the economic ones. Nobody in Europe even pretends that there is the slightest economic need for a single currency. Economic and monetary union between such disparate economies is likely to lead to trouble. Economically backward countries will find that they will lose their most powerful competitive weapon, a flexible currency. They will be locked into a permanently high state of unemployment. More developed countries will find themselves supporting this sorry state of affairs financially. Monetary union cannot happen without massive funds making their way from one part of the European Union to another. The concomitant of that will be an ever more powerful central bureaucracy that will collect and distribute the funds (never forgetting its own advantages) and generally regulate the political and economic life of Western Europe. It is easy to foresee the kind of resentments that situation will lead to. The purpose of the monetary union is political. This has been admitted by all (except the British chancellor of the Exchequer). But unification enforced through economic methods, imposed on an unwilling populace that feels no loyalty to the new entity of the European Union, that has no shared language, culture, or national sentiment, carries within it the seeds of a bloody destruction.

Nations grow closer through shared interests, through free trade, travel, mutual understanding. They grow apart under an imposed political yoke. The Soviet Union, Yugoslavia, and their successor states should serve as warnings. But we do not need to go that far. Nationalistic (as opposed to national) feelings are growing in Western Europe. The common fisheries policy has resulted in battles between French, Spanish, and British fishermen. Resentment of Germany is growing in all the member states of the European Union and is seriously encouraged by Chancellor Kohl's bullying "warnings." The Portuguese, for instance, resent Spanish producers who, protected by the European Community, drive the locals out of the market. One can go on in this vein. Above all, there is the question of democracy and legitimacy. Democratic states with legitimate governments are no threat to their neighbors. An undemocratic, centralized superstate, seething with national resentments, is a potential danger to the world.

United We Fall: Fatal Flaws in the Federalist Case

GERALD FROST

Research director, The New Atlantic Initiative

Is the creation of a federal state the best means by which Europe may achieve a peaceful, stable, and prosperous future? According to Helmut Kohl, the German chancellor, federalism provides not merely the best but the only such means. The alternative vision of Europe's future, that of a collection of independent cooperating states, is, in his view, a dangerous chimera, one that necessarily leads to economic decline and catastrophic war.

The recurring nightmare of a major war—to which those Europeans older than fifty are particularly prone—has sharply accelerated the drive for "ever closer union" since German reunification and the end of the cold war. In Germany itself, that fear partly reflects deep uncertainties about the future conduct of an unconstrained German state. A recent paper from Mr. Kohl's ruling party, the Christian Democratic Union, is remarkably candid on this score, warning that "without this further development of European integration, Germany might be challenged or be tempted on the grounds of its own security needs, to bring about stabilization in eastern Europe alone, and in the traditional manner."

The integrationist logic is seemingly straightforward, if not simplistic: the two worst wars in recorded history began as nationalist conflicts between European states; future catastrophes can therefore be avoided if European states are conjoined in a single entity. It follows that (1) the federalist bonds must be bound tightly—tightly enough to prevent Germany from behaving "in the traditional manner"— and (2) the new political arrangements must be inclusive in character. The problem is that these two aims are incompatible: those who argued that the deepening of Europe would prevent its widening have already been proved right by events. The Central Europeans are still being denied full European Union membership—despite the sincere desire of Chancellor Kohl and many other European leaders to admit them—precisely because political and economic integration has already gone too far for that to be a practical possibility. In Bonn, the talk is now of partial membership or transitional arrangements leading to full membership when the European house has been put in order. But entry will be harder still if and when the final touches to the federalist house have been completed because the processes of political and economic adjustment resulting from new admissions will necessarily be more acute. Moreover, in Britain, opposition to continued membership in the EU is growing as the scope and ambition of the federalist project—and the implications of these for national sovereignty—have gradually penetrated a previously obtuse public consciousness.

A Failure in Logic

The errors in the integrationist logic are amply illustrated in a speech given by Chancellor Kohl at the University of Louvain on February 2, 1996, in which he declared : "There is no reasonable alternative to ever closer integration among European peoples . . . we have no desire to return to the nation-state of old. It cannot solve the problems of the twenty-first century. Nationalism has brought great suffering to our continent—just think of the first fifty years of this century." Present-day Germans were consequently much aware that German unity and European integration were "two sides of one and the same coin," he continued.

Chancellor Kohl's error is to confuse extreme nationalism with the democratic nation-state. This is a mistake of sufficient magnitude to call into question the vastly ambitious project being built on it. For while extreme nationalism is almost guaranteed to produce instability and conflict, the record of the modern democratic nation-state suggests a deep and innate reluctance to initiate aggression in almost any circumstance.

Whether a multinational state would prove to be equally peace loving cannot be predicted. But given the existence among EU members of wide differences in patterns of national economic development, as well as in such matters as language, culture, mores, and systems of law, there are strong grounds for doubting whether it is likely to be as effective in resolving divergent perspectives and interests arising *within* its borders. In the absence of democratic institutions capable of that task, the risk of internal conflict—including that arising from competing nationalisms—must be taken seriously.

The arguments outlined above quite obviously represent a major criticism of German policy, but they are not inherently anti-German. Indeed, they assume a better view of modern Germany than those German politicians who wish to pursue national interests through the EU because they do not trust themselves sufficiently to do so by more direct means. The German distrust of themselves may be hard to live with, but such troubling anxieties would arguably be more satisfactorily assuaged by accepting responsibilities commensurate with Germany's size and importance. The attempt to load those responsibilities on a supranational state with which no automatic identity of interest can reasonably be assumed may, in the end, be more likely to maximize differences between Germany and her neighbors than the opposite. Indeed, the chancellor's dogmatic assurances that no difference can be permitted between Germany's interests and those of the EU are bound to provoke apprehensions that Germany sees the EU merely as the instrument of its will. They are also likely to create the impression that when divergences of interest between Germany and its EU partners do arise, as they inevitably will, Germany will use its preponderance of economic power to steamroll opposition.

Flawed Economic Arguments

If the political arguments for a federal Europe are open to question, the economic ones appear still more deeply flawed. Supporters of a federal Europe customarily argue that unless Europe accepts a greater degree of economic and political integration, it cannot compete with the economic giants, Japan and the United States. This seems implausible: South Korea, Taiwan, Hong Kong, and New Zealand are among the most competitive and fastest-growing world economies but are not part of any political-economic grouping or even of a closely integrated trading bloc. The federalist argument contends that the major economic players are states, rather than companies (an increasing number with an international or global rather than national identity), a view that encourages outmoded mercantilist solutions.

In an increasingly open and liberal international economic environment, the economic task of the state is to provide a sympathetic framework of laws and institutions and to enforce competition. Just how well the EU has been fulfilling that role can be seen in the declining growth rates and the high unemployment rates for almost all EU members. An important indicator of Europe's economic decline can be seen in its falling share of world trade—down 25 percent over the past decade. Another is the fact that as a proportion of industrial output, high tech is one-third greater in Japan and America than in Europe.

Europe also has some of the highest unemployment rates in the developed world, having lost 6 million jobs since 1990. Unemployment in Germany (which has one of the lowest rates) has now reached 4.7 million (nearly 12 percent), equivalent to the population of Norway, and in marked contrast to the low rates that obtained in the former federal republic of the 1960s and 1970s.

The reasons for Europe's economic decline are not difficult to discern. High levels of public spending and borrowing have resulted in high personal and payroll taxes and a consequent lack of industrial competitiveness; these, in turn, discourage inward investment and entrepreneurship. The proportion of wealth consumed by the state among EU members now averages almost 50 percent, compared with 33 percent in the United States and less than 20 percent in the case of the pace-setting Asian tigers.

In addition, centralized decision making, in the form of a ceaseless torrent of regulation from the Brussels Commission, has distorted the market, while the most expensive and least efficient system of agricultural support ever devised—the Common Agricultural Policy—has kept retail food prices high, protected inefficient producers, and accounted for nearly half of the EU budget without slowing the decline in farm income. The only identifiable beneficiaries of the CAP are the bureaucrats who run it, a relatively small number of large landowners, and the criminals who have fraudulently exploited the Kafkaesque rules governing support prices and land set-asides.

Following its undignified departure from the European exchange rate mechanism in 1992, Britain has become the economic success story of Europe; this is largely due to two significant factors. First, once free of the ERM strait jacket, Britain was able to set interest rates on the basis of market realities. Second, uniquely among members of the EU, Britain enjoys exemption from the European Union's social charter: British employers are not obliged to meet heavy costs of labor benefits arising from its provisions. Along with labor market flexibility, this latter factor explains why Britain has attracted a disproportionately large share of inward investment into the EU. The fact that the one EU country presently enjoying bright economic prospects and a good recent record on jobs and growth happens to be the EU member whose integration has gone least far can scarcely be regarded as an advertisement for further integration.

Those nations within the EU that have been forced to recognize the causes of poor economic performance have recently held open the possibility that the tiger will change its spots: decision making will be decentralized, labor markets made more flexible, public spending reduced, taxes cut, competition more keenly encouraged. Alas, this particular tiger is incapable of changing its spots. Its centralizing, regulating, and high-tax ways are, in part, a consequence of the Christian Democratic philosophy that is still influential in much of Europe. But such means are undoubtedly necessary to impose convergence on a remarkably diverse and complex patchwork of states, many at quite different stages of economic development and most of which are keen to retain their separate cultures and identities. If a federal state is to be created, it can be done, if it can be done at all, only by centralized decision making, regulation, and bureaucratic diktat and a judicial system that is intended to promote underlying political goals. Such means, however, are wholly inimical to economic success.

Creating the New Atlantic Community

DANIEL HAMILTON

Associate director, Policy Planning Staff, U.S. Department of State

A new world is upon us. For some, it happened too quickly. They worry that the unifying glue of the cold war has dissolved. They believe that economic challenges and mutual distraction with domestic issues will inevitably weaken the transatlantic partnership, that Europe and America will drift apart.

These are serious concerns and should be treated seriously. But I disagree profoundly with these pessimistic conclusions. They reflect a curious nostalgia for the cold war. They fail to appreciate the enduring fabric of civilization that continues to bind the people of Europe and North America. And they fail to appreciate the serious, if different, security challenges that continue to confront the Atlantic community.

More people have died violently in Europe during the past five years than during the previous fifty. The cold war is over, yet there are greater insecurities in some parts of Europe today than during the entire period of East-West confrontation.

"This post-Communist Europe of ours is rent by a great conflict of two spiritual cultures," the former Polish dissident Adam Michnik warned in 1990. "One of these cultures says, let us join Europe and let us respect European standards, while the other says, let us go back to our own national roots and build an order according to our national particularity."

This tension between liberal and illiberal nationalisms, between forces of integration and fragmentation, has replaced Soviet expansionism as the greatest threat to peace in Europe.

For the first time in its history, Europe has the potential to create a stable order based on shared values of democracy, market economies, and peaceful cooperation. But it could also succumb to the forces of xenophobia and intolerance that exploded so visibly and violently in Bosnia.

It is fair to ask why Europe's troubles should matter much to Americans. Now that the cold war has ended, it is tempting to say that it is time for the Europeans to work this out themselves, while Americans focus on problems at home.

This temptation, while understandable, must be resisted for two simple reasons. The first is our own narrow self-interest. The context for U.S. relations with Europe may have changed, but bedrock American interests in Europe endure: a continent free from domination by any power or combination of powers hostile to the United States; prosperous partners open to our ideas, our goods, and our investments; a community of shared values, extending across as much of Europe as possible, that can facilitate cooperation with the United States on a growing range of global issues; a continent free of the kind of strife that drains inordinate resources from the United States and the rest of the world. These interests require active U.S. engagement in Europe.

The lesson of Bosnia—and the lesson of this century—is that America is a European power, an enduring and essential element of the European balance. Europe without America is unstable. And an unstable Europe threatens vital and enduring American interests.

The question is thus not whether the United States should engage in Europe, but how. That leads to the second reason why we must resist the false prophets of isolation: we have a historic opportunity, only the third such chance in this century, to build a lasting peace in Europe.

A half-century ago, at the end of World War II, the United States faced another time of great change in Europe, another time of enormous opportunity and uncertain peril, another time when Americans wanted nothing more than simply to go home. But we soon found that freedom's wartime victory was incomplete and that the postwar period would require continuous and active American engagement to marshal the forces of freedom for a new kind of war, a cold war.

Among the challenges that Harry Truman, George Marshall, Dean Acheson, and their Democratic colleagues faced was to build a new postwar order in cooperation with a new Republican Congress. And, to the lasting benefit of our nation and the world, they met that challenge. They found allies among Republicans who recalled the consequences of isolationism after World War I—a period that also began with a Democratic president facing new Republican majorities in Congress. They forged a bipartisan consensus based on the Truman Doctrine and the Marshall Plan, the postwar institutions of the West, and sustained American leadership.

Those critics who believe the Atlantic community was nothing more than a creation of the cold war and so will disappear with its end forget that at the end of World War II the United States and its partners set forth a strategic vision based not on one but on two goals: to contain Soviet power and communism from the East and to draw together our allies and former enemies in the West.

During the cold war, attention focused naturally on the first goal—containing the East. But the second goal—revitalizing the West—was equally important, was a precondition for successful achievement of the first goal, and preceded the cold war. The founding of intra-Western institutions—most notably the Bretton Woods institutions, the General Agreement on Tariffs and Trade, the Organization for European Economic Cooperation, and its successor, the Organization for Economic Cooperation and Development—helped to stabilize and liberalize postwar market economies, structure cooperative relations within Europe and across the Atlantic, and promote unprecedented peace and prosperity.

The leaders of the Atlantic community realized that Europe's security could not be based solely on external guarantees; it had to be built from within societies. They knew they would be able to deal with the external challenge from the East only if they could draw effectively on the inner resources of the West. The two goals were mutually reinforcing; the strategic vision was enormously successful.

Now, a half-century later, we must show the same broad vision. Again we have two compatible strategic objectives: first, to integrate eastern democracies rather than contain eastern dictatorships, and second, to build on our achievements by adapting and revitalizing the West. We have the opportunity—and the responsibility—to marshal the forces of freedom for a new kind of European peace, one that is just and enduring. We have the opportunity—and the obligation—to work with our European partners to extend freedom's victory to all Europe, to lock into place the gains of the cold war's demise by building a new Atlantic community geared to the challenges of the twenty-first century.

Our efforts to build this new Atlantic community are based on the recognition that security in Europe today includes, but goes beyond, the military dimension. "The old security was based on the defense of our bloc against another bloc," the president has said. "The new security must be found in Europe's integration—an integration of security forces, of market economies, of national democracies. Combined, these forces are the strongest bulwark against Europe's current dangers—against ethnic conflict, the abuse of human rights, the destabilizing refugee flows, the rise of aggressive regimes and the spread of weapons of mass destruction. . . . I believe our best partner, as we look toward the twenty-first century for prosperity and for peace, is a Europe unified in democracy, in free markets, in common security."

President Clinton's vision builds on five decades of bipartisan support for transatlantic structures of peace on a foundation of European unity. "Our objective," Under Secretary of State Robert Lovett told Averell Harriman in December 1948, "should continue to be the progressively closer integration, both economic and political, of presently free Europe, and eventually of as much of Europe as becomes free."

Lovett's goal is now within our grasp for one simple reason: the singular success of the Atlantic community. The combination of common goals and values and the real integration of our societies, economies, and defenses are the most potent example of shared effort among people ever recorded and the most important impulse to counter the forces of fragmentation that threaten to roil the continent.

The West owes much of its success to the great institutions created in the 1940s and 1950s. These structures offer a usable foundation for a new security architecture. As former secretary of state Warren Christopher said, "These institutions helped produce unparalleled peace and prosperity for half a century—but only for half a continent." Now we have the opportunity—indeed, the necessity—to extend this Europe of institutions to the Europe of the map, to erase forever the dividing line created by the Red Army in the late spring of 1945.

If these institutions were closed to both internal and external adaptation, if they were to remain frozen in their cold war configurations, they would become irrelevant to the post–cold war world. Our common challenge is to maintain their coherence, extend their reach, and reform their structures without diluting their basic functions.

President Clinton's strategy builds on the success and enduring value of these institutions and is based on enlargement, integration, and inclusion. It has six cornerstones:

1. revitalizing the North Atlantic Treaty Organization through internal adaptation, including a greater European visibility and capability within the alliance and a greater ability by NATO to conduct joint operations with nonmembers; external adaptation, including enlargement, the Partnership for Peace, and a new Atlan-

tic Partnership Council; and new roles and missions, as reflected most visibly and dramatically by the role of the Implementation Force (IFOR)—and now the Stabilization Force (SFOR)—in Bosnia

2. integrating Russia into Europe's broad security and economic architecture, including an enhanced NATO-Russia relationship

3. supporting European integration, enlargement of the European Union, and joint U.S.-EU actions in Europe and around the world under the umbrella of the New Transatlantic Agenda

4. strengthening the Organization for Security and Cooperation in Europe, which addresses the root causes of Europe's security challenges

5. encouraging Central and East European states to resolve subregional tensions and consolidate democracy and market reforms

6. engaging Congress and the American people in a broad, bipartisan effort to ensure America's continuing role as a European power

For half a century, the Atlantic community has been the leading force for peace and prosperity—for ourselves and for the world. But, at the threshold of a new century, there is a new world to face—with challenges no less critical than those faced by our counterparts half a century ago. Without a strong new Atlantic community, the prospects for a safer, richer, cleaner, freer world in the coming century will fade. The world is too dangerous, and our opportunities too great, for us to take our partnership for granted.

Europe—Taken by Surprise

WERNER HOLZER

Author, former editor in chief, Frankfurter Rundschau

That is the problem with understanding Europe: the old continent speaks not only with a plethora of languages but with an even greater number of discordant arguments. And the different tongues reflect different histories. To understand the changing moods of the Europeans toward European unity, one must take at least some historical developments into account. That is even more true for Germany than for the other—mostly Western European—countries that are active partners in today's grand experiment.

History aside, most people in the European Union, including the Germans, seem to have one thing in common: all of a sudden, they are getting serious about continental unity. People had become so used to listening to all those impressive speeches delivered by politicians, mostly on Sundays, about the common European dream that they had forgotten to think about consequences. Now they seem to have been taken by surprise. Not only is the European Monetary Union imminent and with it the disappearance of time-honored national currencies, but so is the weakening of many other national institutions. The angry feeling that nobody told them well in advance is widespread even with pro-Europeans. They liked the dream of a strong and united Europe but thought that they had more time to get used to it.

European unity is an old dream—old indeed. Kings, emperors, dictators, and even popes and religious reformers and fanatics have tried their hand at it. The result has been a history of war, conquest, and oppression. In this century, it took two bloody wars to convince people that European unity by democratic consent was a possibility. But even then the idea was not a child of great love of unity but rather a creature of common fear about the future. Realistically, it was not a bad start.

In September 1946, just one year after the end of World War II, one of the great statesmen of Europe in this century, Winston Churchill, a leader with both vision and realism, a man who had led his country to victory in the war and was voted out of office immediately after, had the courage to call for a united Europe in the middle of devastation. Few people listened to the grand old man, and even fewer agreed with him when he spoke up in Zurich, Switzerland. The bloodiest war in this century had left deep scars in the minds and hearts of Germany's neighbors, and Germany had almost destroyed itself by a war the country's leaders had started. How could Churchill ask Germany's wartime enemies—especially France—to offer reconciliation and ask France and the defeated Germans to take the lead in this grand design?

Since the Yalta Conference in February 1945, where he had met Joseph Stalin and Franklin Delano Roosevelt, Churchill had not trusted the Soviet leader, who had been an ally against Hitler during the war. Churchill was afraid that the people of Europe, living in ruins, hungry and without hope, without the strength to help themselves, might fall victim to a new tyranny coming up behind the horizon. Stalin's shadow had already reached East and Central Europe. The iron curtain was coming down even before Churchill gave it that name. The majority of Western Europe's population shared Churchill's fear. It was to become the most powerful push for a new thinking in European terms. And it certainly helped that many, mostly young, people were ready for the idea: French and German students met at their common border and started burning the border barriers between their countries.

German Concerns

This is old history now. The uniting of Europe has come a long way since then—despite the deep wounds of war and the horrors of the Holocaust that had made it so difficult to even think of an integration of West Germany into European structures. But U.S. aid—the Marshall Plan more than anything else—and the growing threats of the cold war made the Western European governments move faster than they originally had planned. One must be realistic: without the division of Germany and the constant confrontation in Berlin and along West Germany's eastern borders, threatening peace not only in Germany but in the whole of Europe, the acceptance of the West Germans would have taken much more time. Mistrust prevailed even while the European Coal and Steel Union came into being. The European Defense Community fell through because of strong resistance in France. Only American leadership in the North Atlantic Treaty Organization made West Germany's integration possible. A French observer in those days gave a mildly cynical definition of the ulterior motive behind the acceptance of Germans into NATO: "First, to keep the Russians out. Second, to keep the Americans in. Third, to keep the Germans down."

The Germans, strangely enough for their new partners, did not bother about the schizophrenic fact that they were wanted and mistrusted at the same time. To be part again of the family of nations was their priority. Their nation-state had been totally discredited by their own chauvinism; it was nothing they cared for much any longer. History does teach lessons once in a while. As an American writer, John Dornberg, wrote in 1960: "Germany—the western part of it—is in a puzzling state of betwixt and between, geographically ripped to pieces, economically powerful, emotionally unstable, respected and feared simultaneously by its neighbors and allies." Thirty-six years later, there is still some truth in this analysis. It explains why a united Europe is more of a hope for Germans than for other Europeans.

France and, even more so, Great Britain have kept much stronger feelings for their own national traditions. For the Germans, there is little left to give up in exchange for Europe's unity—except their strong currency. It might well be that the political miracle of the Franco-German reconciliation has a lot to do with the respect the Germans pay the French for joining them on the train to Europe despite the stronger feelings of the French for their national identity. This holds true even if people west of the Rhine River realize that France has a powerful economic interest in the unity of a Europe that will not be dominated by an economic giant at the eastern border.

Another side to the European coin still is irritating many Germans. As the European Monetary Union draws closer and closer, they feel again betwixt and between in a special way. There are many things for Germans to consider when they look back at their country's history in this century. Above all, they had to live through a traumatic and singular experience twice since the end of World War I: the total ruin of their currency. Remembering this, nobody can be surprised that the strength and stability of the deutsche mark is some kind of an ersatz for the loss of most other identity-building factors.

The idea that a united Europe means giving up their one symbol of success is therefore not greeted with enthusiasm. Some polls during 1995–1996 show Germans' considerable reluctance toward such a sacrifice. All mainstream political parties have underestimated people's fears that the new European currency—whatever it will be called in the end—will not be as stable as their deutsche mark. While the political class on the whole remains steadfast in support of monetary union, a small minority is going the populist way and uses these fears toward their own political goals.

Unlike in other countries, in Germany neither the constitution nor the law of the land requires a plebiscite to ratify monetary union. And neither the coalition government nor the opposition is calling for one. But the political leadership would do well to be much more active in trying to convince the German public that the Eurocurrency is going to be as stable as the deutsche mark. This is all the more necessary in times of recession and deep-reaching changes in the industrial and social structure of the country. Still, few observers believe that a strong political backlash could occur against the decision of an overwhelming multiparty majority in favor of the EMU, even if many Germans are unhappy about the fact that most European institutions still lack democratic control or have little power—like the European Parliament—to exercise control.

National interests and national political decisions will not disappear with the emergence of a common European currency or even with the creation of a more federal setup in Europe—something that will take a lot more time and effort to bring about. As far as American interests are concerned, the EMU does not change the basic economic facts, though it will require procedural changes in dealing with both the new European institutions and the remaining national (regional) structures. Whatever the merits of German politics during the past four decades, there was never any doubt that working hard to foster European integration did not weaken Germany's conviction that Europe must be a reliable pillar in transatlantic relations and not isolate itself from its partners in the United States and Canada. There are no signs that this conviction will change in the foreseeable future.

European Integration and German Interests

OTTO LAMBSDORFF

Member of Parliament, former minister of economics (Germany)

The collapse of the barriers separating eastern and western Germany revived diverse prejudices about Germany in other countries. Reunification was regarded as the first step back to the old Germany with its national, isolationist power politics, stirring up trouble and conflict in Europe. Even notable European politicians held such preconceptions. Hence, it was only natural for me, as a politician who had helped to build the Federal Republic of Germany on new, democratic principles from the ruins of the German Reich, and for many others in Germany to wish that the 2 + 4 Treaty completing German unification should be closely bound up with the commitment to European integration. Germany had to counter these old fears and prejudices by adhering to a confidence-inspiring, pro-European course. Then as now, the concept of a European Union has for Germany paramount geopolitical significance. It is the mainstay ensuring that liberty and democracy, peace and security retain their validity as the fundamental principles of European coexistence. There is no separate course for Germany in Europe, but only the common, European course.

The Economic Foundation

The political standing of the European Union is founded on its economic achievements: the creation of open markets throughout Europe, more effective division of labor, and active involvement in liberalizing trade. These achievements are, moreover, a solid foundation for a community of shared values. Thus, the Maastricht Treaty of 1992 on European Economic and Monetary Union is more than a treaty furthering economic integration. It is tangible proof that even after the end of the cold war and the disappearance of political blocs, the countries of Europe will continue to steer a common course. Hence, it has not been solely the attempt to establish a European counterweight to the Eastern bloc that has brought the countries of Europe together. The long-term objective is to establish political union in Europe on the basis of freedom and democracy. Viewed in this light, the European Union can even serve as an example of a possible form of coexistence among Eastern European countries after the collapse of the Eastern bloc. Nation-states, as they existed before World War I, cannot be models for the future of Central and Eastern Europe. This lasting geopolitical significance should prompt the United States to look favorably on and to support European integration.

Experience has shown us that integration needs a solid economic base, and monetary union, too, will have to lead to a permanent community of stability if Europe is to take shape as a political entity as well. Thus, the participation of countries in the final and decisive stage of monetary union is governed by strict economic criteria. These include limits on public-sector deficits, government debt, price movements, interest rate levels, and exchange rate fluctuations. Not only the problematical state of the economy in Germany but developments in other European countries as well are making it increasingly clear that the goal of introducing the single European currency in 1999 is ambitious. Germany, for instance, the country of the "economic miracle," clearly failed in 1995 to meet the criterion stipulating that the general government deficit may not exceed 3 percent of the gross domestic product. It will be above this limit in 1996 as well. Luxembourg is currently the only country fulfilling all criteria. But there is no cause at present to question the schedule set out in the treaty. To do so would be to invalidate all efforts for reform, most notably those of the French and German governments. Taking away the timetable removes all pressure to comply with the Maastricht criteria.

Germany in particular must be mindful that those who now question the timetable may be suspected of opposing the course of European integration as a whole. Given the political dimension of its economic situation, Germany of all countries should take care not to give the impression of wanting to slink away from the Maastricht Treaty at the first sign of difficulties.

Postponement, should it prove inevitable, would by no means be the end of an integrated Europe. The process of European unification has already had to cope with repeated delays. The economic and integrative effects of the single European market in conjunction with the prospect of completion of economic and monetary union at a later stage are capable of fostering growth and employment in Europe. Should it prove impossible to keep to the deadline agreed in the Maastricht Treaty, I would view this as an added incentive to redouble our efforts to achieve economic convergence and to fulfill the criteria. The European Union takes a similar stance; countries that do not from the outset introduce the single European currency can participate in monetary union at a later date.

But I would caution against prophesying the failure or postponement of economic and monetary union. This could trigger an irrational flight into the deutsche mark on the one hand and to the safe haven of the dollar on the other, which would be neither in the German nor in the American interest. The appreciation of the deutsche mark would strangle Germany's export trade. The deutsche mark is not suited to the role of an international reserve currency. Nor will there be any return to Bretton Woods—an arrangement that came to grief more than twenty years ago. International currency turbulence can be controlled only by consistently pursuing sound economic, fiscal, and tax policies. The adjudicators of European policy are the international financial markets. The structure of a single European currency must be erected on firm foundations. A level-headed and professional approach is needed both in Europe's interest and in view of the geopolitical significance of European integration. Germany stands by Europe. It has the greatest interest in a stable European Union.

Today's Economics

From the German standpoint, there are also well-founded economic reasons in favor of progress on European integration. We are in the midst of a process of structural change. New goods are being produced and new services provided all over the world. The time is long past when Europe and North America alone made up the center of global economic activity. Japan has become a third center. The Southeast Asian tigers are showing us their claws. Latin America is booming. New Zealand and Australia, China, and India must also be mentioned in this context. Eastern Europe is gathering economic strength on the back of reforms. The worldwide shift in production locations is a historically unprecedented process. Capital and private enterprise are becoming increasingly mobile. New telecommunications and transport technologies have brought the countries of the world closer together. All this has had a perceptible impact on Germany, which has always been strongly bound up in the global economy. Germany's locational advantages are rapidly disappearing, if only because the others' are improving. Not only the multinationals think internationally when pricing their production—even Germany's medium and small businesses now do this, especially as cheaper production sites are available next door, in Eastern Europe.

This is the challenge to which politicians must respond. Nowadays, a strategy to promote growth and employment does not imply merely a readiness to carry out a reform of national economic, fiscal, budgetary, social, and wage policies. Germany cannot by itself react to changes in world markets. Isolation is no response to globalization. For Germany to retreat into protectionism and renationalization would be a withdrawal into the "private" sphere that would eclipse the problems rather than solve them. This is one of the reasons I am a European by conviction. European integration has always been, and continues to be, conducive to promoting growth and employment in Germany.

As befits such a complex issue, public debate in Germany encompasses a wide range of views. In a survey of 700 German companies conducted by a leading German economic research institute, one in five respondents said that they expected to be adversely affected by the introduction of a single European currency while two in five expected to see disadvantages for the German economy in general. The Federation of German Industry (BDI) and, to cite a further example, some of Germany's leading commercial banks have issued an urgent appeal for completion of the final stage of economic and monetary union. The German government and the federal president strongly support the introduction of a single European currency and paint a bleak picture of the effects of failure, ranging from currency instability and competitive devaluations to a relapse into nation-state and, by extension, protectionist trade policies. The Deutsche Bundesbank supports the project while stressing the need for strict compliance with the agreed economic criteria. The Social Democrat opposition is divided between rejection of economic and monetary union, as advocated for instance by Oskar Lafontaine, the party chairman and prime minister of the Saarland, and by Gerhard Schröder, the influential prime minister of Lower Saxony, and unequivocal assent by Klaus Hänsch, the Social Democrat president of the European Parliament, by Hans Apel, a former German finance minister, and, above all, by former chancellor Helmut Schmidt. In debating the opportunities and risks of monetary union, the leading economic research institutes and the panel of experts for the assessment of aggregate economic trends, an independent body advising the government, are faced with a trilemma: strict compliance with the economic criteria, strict observance of the timetable, and the demand that as many European member states as possible should participate.

This brief survey of the range of German opinion on economic and monetary union is by no means representative, but it does show that both the economic and the political aspects are taken into consideration. Notwithstanding their apprehension at giving up the deutsche mark, people in Germany are aware of the economic significance and historic dimension of economic and monetary union for Europe, as shown explicitly, and gratifyingly, by the failure of the Social Democratic Party's campaign to exploit anti-Maastricht sentiment in a number of state elections in March 1996. Their anti-European rhetoric led them by way of a resounding setback at the polls directly into parliamentary opposition. People want objective information and matter-of-fact argument. Europe is not a stamping ground for populists. This is good news for Germany and for our partners alike.

The Europe of Berlin

W. R. SMYSER

Author, The German Economy

The leaders of the European Union are moving, slowly but surely, toward a European transcontinental architecture. They are planning to bring the states of Central and Eastern Europe into the European Union. Their plans will ultimately create a European colossus, one that will reach from the Atlantic to the Pripet Marshes and perhaps to the Moskva River.

Such a move will take time. The states that may be first in line, such as Poland, the Czech Republic, and Hungary, will not join until the early part of the twenty-first century. The last states now in line will probably not be admitted until the second or third decade of that century.

But we should not underestimate the importance of the move, no matter how long it may take, for the European Union has set out on a path that will establish the fifth Europe of modern times:

- The first Europe, established in 1648, was the Europe of Westphalia.
- The second Europe, established in 1815, was the Europe of Vienna.
- The third Europe, established in 1919, was the Europe of Versailles.
- The fourth Europe, established in 1945, was the Europe of Yalta.

Now comes the fifth Europe, initiated in 1989 but still in its formative stages. It is named after Berlin because that was the city at which the divided Europe of Yalta collapsed when the people of East Berlin broke down the wall.

The enlarged Europe should also be named after Berlin because the end of the Yalta period means that the world will see a Europe increasingly centered on Berlin. That city, originally the capital of Prussia—a state formally abolished in 1945—will sit at the hub of the new Europe. It will be the center of transport and communications. Ultimately, it will become a center for ideas, for scholarship, and for the mingling of East and West that must take place in the new and wider Europe. Brussels may remain the principal seat of the European Union, but it is too far removed from the newly free states of Europe to serve as a true center.

Unreadiness

The European Union has been firmly committed to enlargement since 1993. More and more Central and East European states have joined the queue for membership. The EU and the East Europeans have begun what they call a structured dialogue to review the main issues and to develop common moves toward enlargement.

The European Union has more on its plate than enlargement, which also goes by the European jargon of widening. The EU must also move toward closer integration of its present members (deepening) on such important matters as a common currency, a common security policy, and a truly single market.

Nor is either Western or Eastern Europe now ready for full enlargement. Economically, the states of the EU had 17 million unemployed in 1995 and may have 20 million unemployed by the year 2000. The major European states performed rather badly in the 1996 World Economic Forum list of competitiveness, with only Great Britain ranking in the top twenty (as fifteenth) while both France and Germany ranked in the twenties. The massive EU social and agricultural subsidy programs can expect a close look and some significant change before enlargement can proceed. That will take time and will involve some dislocation.

The states of Eastern Europe are not ready for economic union either. They have their share of antiquated industries, archaic bureaucracies, and trade-blocking customs regulations. They desperately need new investment. They, like Western European states, must abandon the moat mentality that has long dominated their policies.

Political and historical divides also run deep. While East and West European states have coexisted—either closely or at a distance—for centuries, their societies remain different from each other. They have different traditions, different interests, and different mind-sets. The EU, which prides itself on becoming more than a trading bloc, will prove a difficult melting pot.

Essential Enlargement

But enlargement is essential for both parts of Europe. Without it, the EU risks confining itself to irrelevance as an increasingly insulated and protectionist trading bloc of high privilege and low competitiveness. Eastern Europe risks drifting away from the rest of the world and growing back toward old social and political structures. All Europe needs the bracing touch of a new course and a new structure if it is not to become a museum. Enlargement will provide a better incentive for modernization than Asian competition or American hectoring.

The Europeans must see enlargement in this wider context. As German Foreign Minister Klaus Kinkel said in May 1996, "We cannot leave it to the accountants."

For the United States, the new Europe of Berlin offers a larger and a better partner in global affairs. This may not be evident at first, when the pressures caused by enlargement will force the Europeans to look inward. But the new Europe will ultimately want and even need to play a full role in world affairs, politically and economically. It will then want an open global, political, and economic environment, as the United States does already.

The New Trans-Atlantic Dialogue, initiated in December 1995, offers a good vehicle for Europe and America to begin working together and to see how they can best collaborate to express their common interests.

But the United States will also have to recognize that a wider and larger Europe will not be as willing or perhaps as compelled to follow the American lead on global matters, especially on matters close to Europe itself. This attitude was already evident during the first phase of the Yugoslav dismemberment crisis, when the European states tried hard to formulate a policy deliberately designed to express their own rather than U.S. interests. They failed, but they may try again on other matters. Even when the Europeans do not want to go a different path, their interests may compel them to do so.

The new Europe of Berlin offers great opportunities for all Europeans despite the inevitable pains of adjustment. It also offers great opportunities for the United States. But Washington cannot expect that new Europe to follow the U.S. lead or to accept U.S. wisdom as often as it expected from the smaller European Union. The United States will need to adjust more than in the past, but the final result will be worth the effort.

Needed: A Sense of History

Michael Stürmer
Director, Stiftung Wissenschaft und Politik

Europe's strength is its diversity. An English policeman, a German mechanic, a French cook, and an Italian lover—this is how Europeans would like their Europe to be. *E pluribus unum* is an American ideal, the melting pot. The European idea is rather *suum cuique*, that is, to give to Brussels, to avoid the Euro-jargon of *subsidiarity*, no more than necessary.

Therefore, Europe builders should pause before trying, once again, to square the circle. Much as in the past, today's Europeans are united in loving their differences more than their unity. Throughout the ages, Europe could never be put together by hegemony but only through balance, which, in itself, rests on the recognition of difference. European integration comes as a matter of the mind, while national identity, whether expressed in the Union Jack, the deutsche mark, or the memory of Poland's sufferings, produces a flow of adrenalin.

In this time of globalization and agonizing adaptation across Europe, we should not overlook that the welfare state is still a fortress of nationhood, national governments being rejected or reelected according to their performance in providing comfort and confidence. While Europe is being constructed and reconstructed, it is not so much the Brussels administration that is at stake but the survivability of our democracies. National welfare systems, almost autistic, are at odds with an unforgiving global environment and suffer from adverse demographic conditions throughout Europe. This will be the make-or-break issue for Europe, but also for industrial democracy as we have known it throughout the post–World War II period. Instead of fine-tuning the European unity machine, it may be useful, after the 1989 "all change" orders, to go back to basics and ask that one perennial question, What is so European about the Europeans?

The answers range from history, geography, and economics to the climate, the tradition of Roman law, the crusades, the Renaissance, the Enlightenment, and the Industrial Revolution. Even World Wars I and II, seen in a long perspective, now tend to be interpreted as the most dramatic episode of a long European civil war, indeed,

106

as General de Gaulle put it in 1944, *"la guerre de trente ans de notre siècle."* Most of all, the forty years of the cold war, when Europe was divided between the Soviet land empire and the American sea alliance, contributed to the acceptance of a common destiny.

The end of the cold war, however, far from bringing a European harvest, saw Europe deeply disoriented over its destiny, form, and role in the world. The Western part tried to redefine its internal balance but could find agreement only in striving toward an ever more integrated market, while the poor Eastern relations were uneasily invited to joint the party, please, but not too soon. While the Maastricht Treaty, part 1, rests on the assumption that economic interests and, above all, the common currency of the future will force European countries together, the meandering formulas of Maastricht's part 2, on political union, should make everybody hedge their bets. When it comes to European defense, the bottom line, before Dayton as much as after, is still the North Atlantic Treaty Organization.

Europe is, as Thomas Mann once wrote about his native town of Lubeck, above all *"geistige Lebensform."* This description implies essentially the notion of balance more than the notion of unity, let alone hegemony. Absent a clear and present danger from outside, unlikely to emerge overnight, Europe will probably continue to integrate and merge its economic, technological, and financial energies over time, giving this process appropriate form. But to translate the variable geometries of Europe into an overall political structure resembling a state would, now and for the foreseeable future, not bring the desired results but would endanger even the less ambitious objectives.

Within this broader European dilemma, a specific German one remains: whether in a federal Europe or in the Europe of nation-states, with Germany registering 30 percent of the gross domestic product and population, most neighbors will always fear that they will have to live in Germany's Europe, not in their own. The Germans, meanwhile, do not wish to lose their European dream as they are less sure than most others about their national dream.

The great American vision has been to forge one continental nation. For the Europeans from Oslo to Palermo and from Bristol to Brest, let alone to the Urals, this would be a nightmare. European reality is, at best, unity in diversity. This reality is the charm of Europe but also its predicament. As the prevailing state of mind is not likely to change through political preaching, treaty language, or even the exigencies of a common currency, if Europe is to advance much beyond economic integration, it will require the skills of the gardener more than those of the engineer, favorable weather conditions, and plenty of time.

Europe builders, in the present Intergovernmental Conference as in the ones to follow, will have to blend their grand visions with a sense of time and history. They will also have to practice some rare political virtues, among them modesty, self-restraint, and a sense of proportion.

PART THREE
Defense and Security

INTRODUCTION TO PART THREE

Soon after the fall of the Berlin Wall in November 1989 and Germany's subsequent unification, the raison d'être of the North Atlantic Treaty Organization came, predictably, into question. The cold war was over, the Soviet Union dissolved. Some proclaimed that the era of geo-economics was replacing the era of geopolitics; others argued explicitly (and not for the first time) that the utility of force as a tool of foreign policy had become obsolete. Still others maintained that the creation of a new European security identity would rapidly create new burden sharing and diminish the imperative of American leadership. From the Persian Gulf, to Bosnia, to China and Korea, concrete developments have suggested otherwise. After initial timidity, NATO has begun to open its doors to the young democracies of Central Europe. But questions about Atlantic defense remain salient and pressing, as do concerns about NATO's purpose, structure, costs, and capabilities in a period of new challenges and new threats.

NATO Enlargement: American and European Interests

Paula Dobriansky

Senior international affairs and trade adviser,
Hunton & Williams

Despite the demise of the Soviet Union, the United States retains vital security, economic, political, and cultural stakes in Europe. Enlargement of the North Atlantic Treaty Organization, depending on how it is handled, will determine America's future role in Europe and the overall long-term prospects for European stability. And admitting new Central and Eastern European democracies into NATO is in America's best national security interests.

The most basic American goal is to ensure that Europe is not dominated by a single power or a combination of powers hostile to U.S. national security interests. The United States also needs ready access to European markets, both for investment and for sales of goods and services. These goals are incompatible with an unstable Europe. Moreover, given European geography, history, demography, and politics, it is implausible that Western Europe can successfully insulate itself from chaos and instability in Central and Eastern Europe. Thus, for all practical purposes, European security is indivisible.

Given America's stake in Europe, it is not surprising that, twice in this century, when presented with a major threat to European equilibrium, posed in both instances by Germany, American forces were dispatched, at considerable cost in blood and treasure, to the continent. Following the end of World War II, the United States once again projected its power into Europe to provide deterrence, defense, and reassurance against the Soviet threat. Given the geostrategic importance of Europe, there is no doubt that if the European security environment were to deteriorate again, large-scale U.S. intervention would be required. Such an intervention would be costly. Accordingly, minimizing the probability of such a scenario should be a major priority for American statecraft. Czech President Václav Havel put it well: "I am convinced that the American presence in Europe is still necessary. In the twentieth century, it was not just Europe that paid the price for American isolationism. America itself paid a price. The less it committed itself in the beginning of European conflagrations, the greater the sacrifices it had to make at the end of such conflicts."

NATO is the best institution for advancing and protecting America's national security concerns in Europe. It is America's only institutional bridge to the continent. Through NATO, the United States can best influence and shape the future security architecture of Europe and ensure a stable, peaceful, and prosperous continent. Moreover, we have a unique leadership role in making NATO relevant to the security and political challenges of a post–cold war Europe. As Henry Kissinger aptly put it, "The challenge before the Alliance is to translate common interests into common policies and to create an Atlantic zone of stability in a turbulent world." Only through the alliance's enlargement can we make the West's cold war victory irreversible. This is a historic opportunity, and it must not be missed.

Providing an Anchor

What are the fundamental American and European interests that support NATO enlargement? Given the continuing uncertainty about Russia's intentions and its future conduct, as well as the multitude of other potential sources of instability and conflict, it is in our interest and that of our allies to ensure that the countries of Central Europe obtain a political and security anchor in the European community of nations. To be sure, it is difficult to envision a major military threat facing the new Central and East European democracies in the near future. In view of Russia's continuing transgressions in the "near abroad," the discernable shift to the right in Russia's body politic, and, particularly, Russia's brutal behavior in Chechnya, however, one can be justifiably concerned about Moscow's future military policies.

There is no reason to postpone action until a threat becomes imminent. The Central Europeans want a deterrent against a potential worst-case scenario. Moreover, they want to be safeguarded against Moscow's attempts to wield strong economic and security influence over them.

Outright Russian aggression, whatever its long-term probability, is not the only troublesome scenario for the Central and East European democracies. In the near term, the prospects of democracy taking hold in Russia are doubtful, and the potential for Russian internal disorder has increased. Because of the domestic political turmoil in Russia, most Central European officials fear that chaos and violence are likely. Since Central Europe itself is undergoing a difficult political and economic transition, such instability could be particularly detrimental. NATO, however, can fortify the countries of Central Europe as well as the rest of Europe against an entire range of challenges from the East.

The most common criticism of justifying NATO's enlargement as a hedge against the Russian bear is that it would bring about the very problem it is trying to prevent: it would drive Moscow to adopt the most anti-Western course. Interestingly, the Central European assessment of Russia's behavior differs significantly from the views of some Western pundits. Simply put, Central Europeans think that Russia's opposition to NATO enlargement is triggered not by security concerns over NATO aggression, but rather by a desire to retain strong economic and security influence over Central Europe. This is precisely what the Central European countries are trying to avoid.

At the same time, Central Europeans are more optimistic than many American commentators that Russia will ultimately get over the angst, whatever its source, over NATO's enlargement and that, if handled skillfully, no lasting damage to Russia's democratic development or Russia's relations with the West would be inflicted in the process. Stated differently, Central Europeans do not accept the argument that NATO enlargement would serve as a major policy driver, capable of shaping Moscow's strategic choices. Indeed, the notion that Russia, having lost its empire, being beset by economic, political, and demographic problems of every stripe, and running a substantial risk of further fragmentation, would make its most fundamental strategic choice—the nature of its relationship with the West—based on whether or not NATO enlarges itself, is so absurd that to state it is to rebut it.

Even aside from any Russia-related contingencies, the newly established Central and East European democracies express justifiable apprehension about the prospects for internal, regional, and cross-border conflicts and their spillover regionwide. Given the paramount American interest in regional stability, these concerns are worthy of our attention. Long-standing ethnic and religious tensions and social upheavals resulting from refugee flows can prompt instability and even violence. The events that have been transpiring over the past several years in Bosnia and South-Central Europe offer ample evidence that these concerns are not academic. Expanded

NATO membership will ameliorate these regional conflicts. For example, while not quelling all tensions among its members, NATO has effectively restrained Greece and Turkey in their confrontation over Cyprus.

Another strategic concern with impact on our core interests in Europe is the existence of a post–cold war security vacuum between Germany and Russia. As history has proved, such circumstances can spawn dangerous behavior and unholy alliances. In the absence of NATO enlargement into Central Europe and the concomitant continuation of the current security vacuum and potential instability in the region, Germany would have a tremendous temptation to enter into an arrangement with Russia, and Moscow would be certain to exploit it. This apprehension is reenforced by the fact that, ironically, the collapse of the Soviet Union and Russia's current military weakness have fostered both a new agility in Russia's foreign policy and Western susceptibility to it. One can argue that these apprehensions ignore real transformations in German national character and aspirations that have arisen since World War II, yet they cannot be dismissed entirely.

Last but not least, prompt NATO enlargement will have an extremely positive effect on domestic developments in various Central and East European countries. In that regard, one would do well to recall that NATO always dispensed more than just deterrence and defense. Its equally important function was reassuring its members by providing a shared set of institutions and values and a sense of belonging to a broader community. There is no doubt, for example, that NATO membership played a major role in shaping the transformation of Germany from a defeated aggressor of World War II to a successful and economically prosperous democracy. (Arguably, it is precisely because of Germany's unique experience that it has been the strongest European supporter of NATO enlargement.)

In order to cement Central Europe's economic and democratic reforms and buffer them against instability, the United States and Europe should want these countries to develop a closer association with other democracies. Through alliance membership, Central Europe can be instilled with a sense of security, enabling them to thrive and prosper. As former Polish Foreign Minister Bartoszewski said, "The dynamic growth of transatlantic contacts has become possible due to the safe and well-integrated environment created by NATO. Enlargement will produce similar effects in Central Europe."

Alternatives

Are there viable policy alternatives to NATO enlargement? The most frequently invoked candidate is the Partnership for Peace arrangement devised by the Clinton administration primarily as a way of assuaging Moscow's concerns about prompt NATO enlargement. Perhaps the PFP's pedigree should not be held against it, however. Indeed, some analysts argue that, given an objective analysis of threats and challenges facing Central European countries, the Partnership for Peace arrangement meets their concerns. So why not delay NATO expansion? Unfortunately, the PFP is simply unable to deliver to the Central and East Europeans the kinds of deterrence-, defense-, and reassurance-related benefits that they seek.

To begin with, PFP does not distinguish between the state of democratic development and economic reforms of each member country. Rather, they are put on par with one another. The PFP provides no security guarantees, and it places Poland, Hungary, Estonia, and other East European countries in the same pool with Russia, whose intentions concern the others. Finally, for better or worse, perceptions are nine-tenths of reality in international politics. All concerned parties—Russians, Central Europeans, and Americans—when candid, believe that there is something unique about NATO, but not about the PFP.

Aside from PFP, there are no other viable institutional alternatives to NATO enlargement. Essentially, there are two fundamental problems with such contenders as the Western European Union or the European Community. To begin with, because the United States is not a member in these exclusively European institutions, they do not sufficiently engage the United States, thereby greatly detracting from their security and reassurance value. The second problem is that the pace of admission into the more credible institution—the EC—is likely to be quite slow and driven mostly by economic imperatives. Whatever the problems inhibiting early NATO enlargement, the obstacles associated with early EC enlargement are even more formidable. Thus, at the end of the day, NATO enlargement represents the only viable policy option; the only alternative is to do nothing.

Security of Nonmembers

In considering NATO enlargement, one must also analyze its impact on several countries that have yet to express an interest in NATO membership, yet whose independence and security exert important stabilizing influences. Indeed, one of the arguments used by the opponents of NATO enlargement is that the security of countries that are not NATO members would sharply deteriorate because Moscow would conclude that it was free to meddle in their affairs. NATO enlargement, however, if properly pursued, need not jeopardize the security of nonmember countries. Indeed, it should even bolster their security. The most important of such countries is Ukraine, a state the size of France with a population of 52 million. It is geostrategically important to the United States and the West. In fact, it has been described as the "linchpin of European security." Consequently, Ukraine's independence must be solidified.

An important U.S. policy challenge is how to expand NATO without alienating Ukraine. It is imperative to reassure Ukraine that NATO enlargement is an inclusive, not exclusive, process that Ukraine may join if it desires and if it has met established criteria. Moreover, we must communicate clearly that Ukraine is not in a Russian sphere of influence and that, like all the Central European countries, it has an assured future in the European community of nations. Efforts should be maintained to continue vigorous political, economic, and military cooperation at all levels with Ukraine.

Still, given Ukrainian concerns and the importance of Ukrainian independence to American security interests, a key question to address is: Is Ukraine in so precarious a position that it warrants not expanding NATO? The simple answer is no. Ukraine's future, however, must be a significant factor in any strategy to restructure Europe's security landscape. This means that the enlargement of NATO must be accompanied by measures that will reenforce Ukraine's political, economic, and military attachment to the Western community.

In conclusion, the United States has core security, economic, political, and cultural interests in Europe. Our interests can be best achieved through NATO expansion. Significantly, an objective analysis of Central and East European and Ukrainian concerns provides a compelling case in favor of NATO enlargement. After decades of trying to unite the European community of nations and eliminate instability on the continent of Europe, we are within striking distance of this goal. It would be tragic if, instead, we snatched defeat from the jaws of victory.

German Interests in a Changing Europe

CHRISTIAN HACKE

Professor, University of the Armed Forces, Hamburg

The reestablishment of German sovereignty and unity, the end of the East-West conflict, and the collapse of Soviet imperialism have, as with the reestablishment of nation-states in Central and Eastern Europe, changed the framework of German foreign policy. New tensions may arise due to Germany's close ties to the West and the new, geopolitically central position of the unified Germany within Europe. As a result, the question of German interests is increasingly important. This urgency is legitimate, and yet any call for national interest is still viewed critically in Germany, for many Germans associate the notion of national interest with a return to national arrogance and power politics. Considering Germany's past, such concerns are clearly understandable. While Otto von Bismarck was able to employ the notion of national interests cleverly to justify the need of German power, the concept of national interest found itself on a steep decline under his successors, eventually leading to racist and destructive politics in 1933. Against this background, any notions of national interest seemed inappropriate after 1945.

In stark contrast, the Western ties to the Federal Republic led in the ensuing four decades to a multilateralization of German foreign policy, establishing a genuinely new and valuable tradition for the foreign policy of the Federal Republic. The nation was demonized; the integration of Europe, idealized. And at the same time, the traditional definition of power underlying German foreign policy was removed and replaced with notions of responsibility and peace politics.

German Interests since Unification

The unification of Germany in 1989–1990, a period marked by the renaissance of the nation-state and the decline of global ideology, has altered German interests and the constellation of German ideas. The nation has to face new challenges in its foreign policy, while at the same time the expectations placed upon Germany have increased. It is therefore evident that German international interests will have to be reformulated. In hindsight it becomes quite clear that the for-

118

eign policy interests of Germany will be defined by different partners and different foreign states.

To deny that German policy bases itself on the interests of the nation would be wrong. No one has expressed this idea more clearly than Bundespresident Roman Herzog in his speech on the fortieth anniversary of the German Society for Foreign Policy, for as he stated:

> German interests, those are primarily our immediate national interests such as security and preservation of prosperity. It makes no sense to want to hide such things. Our partners would never believe that we bear only international altruism as a shield. Thus for the sake of honesty, it is particularly important to admit that we support such things as a free global market, since they lie within our own interests. German usage of a rhetoric founded on excuses, which allowed the nation to shirk the definition of national interests, was previously understandable considering German aversion to national and interest-oriented rhetoric. Such avoidance, however, is problematic today, for it prevents us from redefining German national interests, which has become essential in recent years.

Today, Germany is surrounded by friends and partners. Century-old rivalries have been buried. Germany has been integrated into the community of Western democratic states, and since the collapse of communism and ideological differences, new spheres of action are being opened to the East. What effect does this have on the definition of German international interests? It is not an easy question to answer, since there are so many different hierarchies of interests, and the deeper one delves into detail, the greater the influence of distinct frameworks and factors in determining Germany's interests.

The primary interest is the securing of German welfare; its citizenry and territory; its political, economic, and social state; community, fundamentals of living, and the proven government system—such institutions and values found the basis of domestic politics and the core of international interests. As such, foreign policy is the pursuit of domestic politics with other means and other stipulations. And yet, in contrast, the attitude German citizens maintain toward the fundamental question of foreign politics is crucial to defining Germany's international interests, for its central interest must rest on the broadest consensus.

As such, Germany's foreign policy interests are defined by the following factors:

- its geographic and geopolitical position in the middle of Europe
- its past
- the attitudes of its neighbors and partners
- the evolution of world politics
- the values represented in statutes
- the conceptualized considerations and the foreign political interests of the government
- the citizens' attitude toward the fundamental questions of foreign policy

While neither the federal government nor the foreign service has previously submitted a comprehensive conceptualization of its interests, the White Book of 1994 gives some insight into the structure of the nation's interests. It states:

> German politics concerning foreign affairs and national security is spurred by five central interests: preserving the freedom, security, and welfare of German citizens and the intactness of the nation's territory; integrating into the European Union with European democracies . . . ; maintaining a lasting relationship with the United States as a world power, based upon common values and interests . . . ; pursuing the goal of binding our Eastern neighbors to Western structures to ensure equalization and partnership and establishing a new security arrangement which includes all European states; and finally, upholding global concern for the rights of individuals and humanity and a global economic order based on the rules of the market economy.

Dialogue, cooperation, defensive preparation, and multilateralism are therefore the chief instruments of the politics that strive to establish a balance between values and interests. If one transforms these interests into concrete principles of action within German foreign policy, the following picture emerges:

- Germany and its citizens safeguarding themselves against external danger and political repression

- prevention, arrest, and termination of crises and conflicts that could injure the totality and stability of Germany and its allies
- extension of the north Atlantic bond of security with the United States, which is based on the similar values and interests of the two nations
- strengthening of the North Atlantic Treaty Organization (NATO) as the protector of common values and defenses of the Euro-Atlantic democracies and extension of such ties to the East
- a balanced partnership between a united Europe and North America
- deepening of European integration through the extension of the European Union (EU) with a common policy for security issues and foreign affairs and a European security and defense identity
- expansion of the membership of the European Union and the Western European Union (WEU)
- strengthening the role of the United Nations in solving global conflicts and strengthening the Organization for Security and Co-operation in Europe (OSCE)
- establishment of a new cooperative security order among all OSCE members
- consolidation and extension of regionally and globally operative security orders based on organizations that strengthen and augment one another
- with the objective of forming a cooperative security order as the basis for lasting peace and stability in and for Europe, Germany's continued promotion of forward-looking conflict prevention emphasizing arms reduction
- promotion of democratization and economic and social advancement in Europe and across the globe

Globalization of German foreign policy requires a differentiated analysis and evaluation of German interests, heeding global, regional, and narrowly defined political viewpoints. The goals and tools of politics must, in relation to one another, be clearly worked out. Only then will German citizens gain an understanding of their nation's foreign policy issues, allowing a German foreign political culture to emerge that promotes the varied interests and brings with it the necessary domestic political discussions. Yet the domestic discussion of German international interests is inadequate because the federal government does not spur the discussion of foreign policy often enough. One cannot escape the feeling that many Germans consider their country a paradise island. As a result of the deficient interest in foreign politics and the increasing concentration on domestic issues, a void of comprehension has emerged, which is harmful not only for the political culture of Germany but also for the complex reciprocal relationships between state and society and between domestic and foreign politics.

Foreign policy must remain public and democratically pluralistic. Although it will be implemented by the executive, foreign policy must be discussed more thoroughly within Parliament than previously. The German government has failed to clarify the risks and dangers of the increasing globalization of its interests.

The Primacy of Interwoven Interests

The interdependent nature of international politics, especially in the global economy, promotes accommodation and cooperation, particularly by nations that, like the Federal Republic, are characterized by many international ties and a high degree of dependence. As such, it becomes ever more difficult to define national interests. Some interests have to be defined as communal, others as primarily national. But more important, integration of politics cannot be idealized as if it were a process in which power and national interests will no longer play a role. In reality, individual states try to exert national influence on international politics and the communal institutions. For although one might be increasingly able to formulate the objectives of the European Union as transnational and supranational, the motives and orientation of individual member states truly emerge from national perspectives. Nevertheless, it remains important to differentiate between actions based on national interests and those based on supranational interests. More vigorously than before, individual policies have to be analyzed to discern the different interests of the individual European states. For supranational arrangements, whether economic, financial, military, or political, truly reveal themselves only when all states follow the same line of policy, even when these steps meet their own national interests.

The principle of interwoven national interests continues to direct the analysis of German foreign policy. Yet these interconnections have to be analyzed separately from time to time to determine how they each affect the national interest. Examined separately, the individual strands of "interwoven interests" give us a clearer understanding of national interests. For even in an integrated Europe, security policies (which were historically and politically the domain of the nation-state) of all member-nations remain chiefly national at the core.

Thus, today the key question is which national interests concerning foreign politics will be communalized. Germany cannot merely highlight abstract values such as freedom, human rights, and political unity in the presentation of its policies but must focus more clearly and concretely on its own interests. Hans-Peter Schwartz has expressed this distinguishing point: "It isn't a question of whether the nation state will dissolve itself, but rather which of its responsibilities it can communalize without risking the democracy and welfare of its own citizens."

How much autonomy does Germany want to hand over to multilateral organizations? How much foreign policy should reflect strictly national interests? The problems of European security have suddenly increased, without a corresponding ability to solve them by common multilateral foreign policies. The German Federal Republic has been particularly affected by the apparent decline of multilateral foreign policy decision-making processes, for the core of its own policies builds on such multilateralism.

Positioned in the center of Europe, Germany depends on functioning multilateral arrangements. Due to its leadership role in the development of foreign policy, Germany has perhaps protected some neighboring states from renationalizing tendencies and exaggerated protection of national interests. But the past five years have revealed that multilateral foreign policy is not sustainable, not even in Western Europe any longer. Crises and wars have since strengthened renationalizing tendencies.

German foreign policy of the previous years was not rooted in the traditional sense of power but built on diplomatic and economic strength. As a result, a complex interdependence between political will and power has remained central to German policies. This is especially true for the communally oriented foreign policy of Germany.

Germany cannot hide behind the joint politics of integration, when this formula is forced to cover up common mistakes and failures, such as with the Western failure in the Balkans. The communal institutions and commencement of integration have not passed their tests, considering recent crises and wars. The principle of "interlocking institutions" such as the United Nations, OSCE, NATO, WEU, and EU failed miserably in the Balkans and dramatically diminished the superiority of the West and of the free world. Thus, communal institutions and the principle of multilateral foreign policy find themselves in a deep crisis. Flights into national egotism, such as through the decline of political accountability and culture, are signals of decline and weaknesses but are not alternatives to multilateralism in international politics.

The Key Roles of German Foreign Policy

The question remains: How will German foreign policy reform itself? Considering the restricted spheres of German influence, this question can be answered only by pointing toward Germany's strong points, specifically its key roles in international politics. The structure of German interests will be determined by its roles as a civil power and as an economic state.

Germany as a Civil Power. Cooperation, integration, and multilateralism have been the cornerstone of German diplomacy and the basis for defining Germany's role as a civil power. Its special role in foreign policy lies in being "the initiator and motor of cooperation with the objective of civilizing international relations." To that end, German foreign policy has geared itself toward institutionalization, justification, and cooperation.

Germany as an Economic State. Already in 1969, Helmut Schmidt had defined Germany's role in the global economic market as that of a superpower. In the triad of the United States, Japan, and Europe, Germany continues to be preeminently an exporter. Yet Germany at the same time depends on imports from the global economic market and not only for raw materials. In contrast to Japan, however, Germany is regionally tied to Europe: over half its exports go to countries in the European Union. In the coming decade, Germany will become more than an economic power within the triad. After unification, Germany took, in regard to economics, neither a national nor a global superpower attitude. In contrast, Germany is a model state in terms of trade and security, but in regard to safeguarding its international interests, it no longer suffices Germany to be only an economic and civil example. Thus, Germany's role in security issues is becoming ever more important.

Germany's Role in Security Issues. For more than thirty years, the armed forces defended a community of nations that, in a competition with communism, proved itself the stronger power. During the period of the East-West conflict, war in Europe was definitely imaginable but not very likely. Until 1989, military strength was considered subordinate, almost as if it were an abstract insurance policy. Yet today, it has achieved real meaning as the collapse of Soviet imperialism has brought with it crises and wars that have to be addressed and, more specifically, ended. In this context, Germany must expand its involvement in security issues and cannot afford to isolate itself from its allies as military solidarity and defensive positions are being established. The necessary integration of German security policies also means taking on larger military responsibilities. For although German security, with the end of the cold war, is more assured than previously, this condition could alter very quickly. The war in the Balkans has clearly revealed that Germany must develop an interest in security issues that extends beyond collective self-defense.

The central duty of the armed forces will continue to be defending the country. But Germany cannot allow itself to be overtaken strategically, psychologically, or materially. The crises and wars in Germany's vicinity have to be contained, to ensure that aggressive nationalism and ethnic and religious fanaticism will not continue to spread to the areas surrounding the country. For that reason, the military forces of East European nations have to be brought into line with the example of Western defense policies as quickly as possible. For the armed forces of the unstable democracies of Central and Eastern Europe are attracted to the concept of "internal command," focusing on such ideas as "uniformed citizens" as the primary tools of the armed forces' defensive and political alliances. Germany must further such cooperative sentiments since long-term stability is possibly the most important contribution that Germany and its armed forces can make toward the security structure of Europe.

Germany's Role in Easing Tensions

Germany's growing reputation in Central and Eastern Europe results primarily from its role in easing tensions in Europe. The negotiations concerning Eastern Europe in the 1970s and 1980s particularly contributed to this role. A unified Germany can build on this tradition by recognizing its political interests in the East. A new political concept for Central and Eastern Europe is, however, required with the region's completely transformed landscape. Adjusting to this new environment is perhaps the greatest challenge in conceptualizing Germany's interests.

Germany as the Instigator of West European Integration

The EU offers the optimal framework for German interests, since economic prosperity and liberal democratic evolution of state and society concurrently foster safeguards against a return to nationalistic tendencies. Yet Germany is the only nation that must deal with reforming Western political, state, and social structures while at the same time overcoming the effects of Soviet domination, dictatorship, and state socialism. It is, therefore, extremely difficult to establish a measured definition of national interests for Germany. No other country has to define its role and interests in foreign politics so close to the intersection of Eastern and Western evolutions. Only Germany is part of the West and at the same time the testing field for the results of the collapse of communism and planned economies. Thus it is essential that the ties to the West be solidified; those to the East, strengthened; and those to the globe, expanded.

Conclusion

Since 1990, a completely new nation-state has emerged, not just a new Federal Republic. New experiences have engendered new values. The political culture and spectrum of the unified Germany will be more diverse and tension filled than the culture of the previous Federal Republic.

Nationhood, national unity, and national identity are still unusual for the Germans, and yet the recognition of their existence is a prerequisite for the definition of national interests. German skepticism about the nation-state means risk as well as opportunity. The risk lies in Germany's insufficient sense of identity in comparison with its neighbors. Opportunity exists in the realization that through the process of unification national interests make sense only when connected with universal values and have to be followed cooperatively. The formula established by Thomas Mann, which was often quoted by the former foreign minister Hans-Dietrich Genscher, of a "European Germany" points to the wish to balance national and European interests.

Until 1945, the failure of a liberal democratic and humanitarian vision led German politics to a fate of violence and oppression. In comparison with other West European and North American democracies, Germany lacked a vital and attractive vision for its foreign policy based on universal standards. But this situation changed in 1949. Germany's exemplary foreign policies, in the tradition of Hans-Dietrich Genscher, are well-regarded around the world. Yet model behavior based on the politics of freedom alone is not sufficient today. What is missing is a foreign policy identity, in which a balance is struck between power and ethics, between accountability and interests, and between spheres of national action and global responsibilities. A skillful diplomacy, based on the notion of using military might only in the last instance to ensure freedom, self-determination, and security, is indispensable: "The use of force doesn't ruin man; it is rather through the use of unlawful violence and through the submission to power which is held as tyrannical, that this occurs."

Helmuth Plesser characterized Bismarck's German Reich as a superpower without a concept of state. The Germans wanted to become a nation, since all others were. Today, Germany has not only become a nation because others are but also because Germany has within the past four decades tied the idea of nation to a supranational ideal. It has assumed the role of a civil power, an economic state, and a mediator in the context of fostering a free democratic civilization based on Atlantic standards. For the first time in its history, Germany in its entirety is a part of the West, part of a bigger civilization into which the legacy of nineteenth-century global humanism has been interwoven. It is the maintenance and extension of these values that remain the indispensable standard on which German national interests must be formulated.

A Receding Horizon: Europe's Attempt at a Common Foreign and Security Policy

JOSEF JOFFE
Editorial page editor and columnist, Süddeutsche Zeitung

One of the pillars of the fabled Maastricht Treaty, right next to monetary union, is the Common Foreign and Security Policy. In English, the acronym for this unwieldy concept is CFSP; in German, the abbreviation reads GASP. *Gasp,* though an accidental pun, is a nice way of framing the issue. The term evokes choking, panting, wheezing, helplessness—in short, a whole array of difficulties. This is a telling definition of the problems Europe has encountered while trying to formulate a common policy in matters of diplomacy and defense.

Klaus Kinkel, the German foreign minister, has defined that ambition: "We want majority decisions [in the European Union], above all in the Common Foreign and Security Policy."[1] It sounds like a simple goal. But, if realized, the CFSP would signal a most profound break in the history of statecraft since the likes of Richelieu and Bismarck formulated the essential tenets of *raison d'état.*

Sovereignty

Reason of state knows no other moral law than necessity and no higher authority than the state. It is chained to another enduring imperative of the state system: sovereignty. Sovereignty means, at least in the normative sense, that the state, and no supra- or subnational institution, shall have the last word in the intercourse with other states. Sovereignty's embodiment is the veto, such as that retained by the five permanent members of the United Nations Security Council. Hence it is the very opposite of decision by majority. In such a setting, state A would stand ready to submit to the wills of states B, C, D, etc. In other words, A would yield the very essence of statehood.

Nowhere has sovereignty demanded more deference than in the realm of foreign and security policy. Even the most rigorous alliance compacts contain an invisible opt-out clause. It reads more or less as follows: "I will honor my obligations, but in the moment of truth, I reserve the right not to discharge them." The ultimate arbiter is the *sacro egoismo* of nations, and it will follow not obligation but reason of state as it, and only it, sees it.

Will the members of the European Union yield their sovereignty for the sake of Europe? Bismarck once scribbled in the margin of a letter from the Russian chancellor Gorchakov: *Qui parle d'Europe à tort; notion geographique*—whosoever talks about Europe is wrong;

---

1. In an interview with the author, "Die letzte Entscheidung muss bei der Regierung bleiben," *Süddeutsche Zeitung,* March 7, 1996, p. 10. All subsequent quotes are taken from this same interview.

merely a geographical notion. True, that was in 1868, during the classic age of cabinet diplomacy and realpolitik. Neither Klaus Kinkel nor Jacques Chirac, the French president, would today admit to the cynicism that Bismarck so freely preached.

Since then, Europe has become much more than a mere geographical notion. It is no longer just the sum of the fifteen EU member-states. In many ways, these states have shared, relinquished, collectivized sovereignty. They submit to the verdicts of the European Court. They allow Brussels to dictate the shape and price of bananas their citizens may ingest. They have opened their borders to EU-wide competition, even where it comes to government procurement.

So why not share or relinquish sovereignty in foreign and security policy, though it is the most impenetrable bastion of sovereignty? The most interesting answer is given by none other than CFSP aficionado Klaus Kinkel: "In defense policy, there will be no majority decision." Doesn't this principle unhinge the very idea of CFSP? His reply: "Majority decision in foreign policy, yes; in defense policy, no." This was too subtle a distinction, interjected the interviewer. Kinkel repeated the point: "We cannot have majority decisions on central issues of defense policy." And what is a central issue? "For instance, the use of military forces." So where would Mr. Kinkel submit to a majority? "For instance, where the EU were to decide about the diplomatic recognition of another state." That is indeed not a central issue.

The Whole More than Its Parts

Q.E.D., the Euro-skeptic would interject at this point. Though Bismarck is dead, he would have used the same language—as would Richelieu. To be sure, states have always yielded (actually, lent) pieces of autonomy to others—in hundreds of treaties where A promised this, and B pledged that. But yielding autonomy temporarily is not the same as alienating sovereignty, which, by definition, cannot be shared. *All* compacts contain the small print *rebus sic stantibus*—provided that things remain what they are. And the parties to the compact have always reserved for themselves to determine whether things had changed or not, above all in matters of war and peace.

Nor would any state, neither France nor Germany, yield this right today. Hence, even Mr. Kinkel, a CFSP advocate, only followed standard procedure when he used different words for affirming the ultimate precedence of the nation state: "No majority decision when it comes to the use of armed forces." Once this claim is made, though (and it would be uttered by *all* members of the European Union), CFSP begins to gasp and wheeze.

Some recent examples dramatize the point precisely because they are far less momentous than war and peace. France, in 1995, continued to test its nuclear devices in the Pacific despite widespread EU opposition. Germany refused to countenance any interference in its Iran policy; what Bonn calls the "critical dialogue" with Tehran was sacrosanct. France consulted nobody when its foreign minister Herve de Charette rushed off to mediate between Israel and Syria and Lebanon during the Operation Grapes of Wrath in 1996. In short, if CFSP does not work in lesser realms, how would *e pluribus unum* arise when core interests come to the fore?

What is left? Above all, a beautiful theory that is hard to gainsay. In manifold variation, the theory runs like this: Europe has to grow into an entity where the whole is more than the sum of the parts. Only in this manner could the European Union finally take its rightful place alongside the great powers like the United States, exerting the influence that its size, population, and economic clout warrant.

That is the lofty ambition; the reality was nowhere more starkly deficient than in the Balkan wars that began in Slovenia in 1991 and ended, for the time being, at Dayton in 1995. In the beginning, the European Union was so confident that the foreign minister of Luxembourg told the United States (in so many words), "This is our war, hands off." The CFSP that the European Union subsequently enacted turned into a sad travesty.

The Germans stayed out of the war *ab initio*, claiming that their Nazi past, especially in the Yugoslav theater, forbade any military intervention. Britain and France did deploy their forces, not in the name of Europe, however, but under the blue flag of the United Nations. In other words, the war was prosecuted in New York, under the watchful eyes of the five veto powers, among which Russia acted as a tacit protector of the Serbs. Paralyzed militarily, the EU was hardly equipped to mediate diplomatically, for example, in the guise of EU emissary Lord Owen. The reason for failure was articulated more than three hundred years ago by Thomas Hobbes: Covenants without swords are but words.

Success came only when, at last, the United States intervened—a real power with the requisite will and hardware. The U.S. emissary Richard Holbrooke could at last bring into play what Europe did not have: a single decision-making center that could mobilize the appropriate means—that could not only cajole but also deter and compel. Theoretically, however, the Europeans could have mustered the necessary wherewithal, too. So why did they fail?

Because the European Union is not the United States of Europe. Because each member-state is driven by its own fears and interests. Because there is nobody who could fuse the many into the one. France will not yield to German leadership, and neither France nor Germany will submit to Britain. They are too "equal," as it were. For every one of them, it is easier to submit to a real superpower like the United States than to one of their own. If there is leadership, it is leadership by committee, and such bodies tend to gravitate to the lowest common denominator, the very enemy of decisiveness and dispatch.

Another example in point: France abolished conscription in 1996, Germany is adamant about its retention. Or take the old tug of war over Europe's "defense identity." France continues to hanker after a purely European defense; Germany and Britain have just as doggedly insisted on an Atlantic link to the United States. Spain and Italy? The rest of Europe does not know, and they themselves probably do not know, either.

It stands to reason that CFSP, a central point on the agenda of Europe's post-Maastricht deliberations, will not generate more than an analysis and planning body that would assist the commission or the Council of Ministers or both. Such an institution will surely help. It will keep a searching eye on the world and furnish its masters with astute analyses and compelling action memoranda. Yet each paper will surely end with a proviso such as "If the governments so desire."

Former secretary of state Henry Kissinger once asked whom he would have to call in Europe in a crisis. There is an obvious theoretical answer. It would be nice to have a European foreign minister, with his own fax and phone number. But there is nobody in Europe, even today, more than a century after Bismarck, who would qualify for this job in the eyes of the fifteen national foreign ministers. They do not wish to vote themselves out of existence. Let us again quote Mr. Kinkel: "A kind of European foreign minister is out of the question for me." Why? "Because the Council of Ministers, i.e., the governments, must have the last word." Richelieu and Bismarck would agree.

A Case for Leadership

BURKHARD KOCH

Managing director, Europa Associates Inc.

NATO is expected to announce in July 1997 the names of the countries with which it *intends* to *start* enlargement talks. The alliance is still slow to chart a clear and purposeful strategy toward East Central Europe. After the initial euphoria about an Eastern Europe quickly reinvented on the Western model, the West realized that it had entered a gray period of uncertainty. Whereas the potential central axis of conflict in Europe during the cold war was along the former inner German border, Europe's post–cold war division runs between the zone of integration, peace, and democracy in the western part of the continent, and the zone of turmoil, fragmentation, and development in its east. Uncertainty about how to transform the North Atlantic Treaty Organization to reflect these changes since the cold war ended went up, confidence in the alliance's institutions declined.

Biding Time

Partnership for Peace was an attempt to win time—time for the West to restructure the Atlantic military alliance for the challenges of a new era; time for the states of Central and Eastern Europe to lay the groundwork to become liberal democracies; time for Russia to adjust herself to her new situation.

During the initial period of euphoria after the breakdown of communism, proposals to dismantle both NATO and the Warsaw Pact were fashionable. There were overly optimistic predictions about how smoothly and quickly former Communist dictatorships might become westernized. In an entirely democratic Europe from the Atlantic to the Ural, there is no need for a military alliance, the argument ran. Indeed, market reform and democratization are crucial factors for shaping a country's behavior beyond its borders. Nowadays, even the mainly leftist proponents of this idea are worried about mothballing the Atlantic alliance before anything meaningful can replace it.

On the other side of the spectrum, political realists, together with unreconstructed cold warriors, thought that after the cold war a strategic vacuum had developed in the heart of Europe, between Germany and Russia. If NATO did not fill it, either an inherently expansionist Russia or a more assertive Germany would do it. NATO's purpose was seen as unchanged: keep the Americans in, the Russians out, and the Germans down. This scenario has not much to do with the interests of those former Warsaw Pact members who are knocking at NATO's doors.

Since 1989, the contradictory judgments have changed as the misperceptions of post-Communist developments have changed as well, finding some common ground:

• The NATO alliance has to become more flexible and less focused on East-West confrontations. NATO has to change significantly so it can deal with the chaos and anarchy that have replaced the Soviet threat. Unless the alliance does not export stability, instability will spill into Western Europe, first into Germany.

• The cold war was about containing the threat of Soviet communism and establishing a democratic zone of peace in Europe. A post–cold war strategy should shield East Central Europe so that it can recover economically, build stable democracies, becoming in this process a cohesive buffer zone against national rivalries, chaos, and anarchy as well as a magnet that will subsequently and ultimately draw the countries of South Eastern and Eastern Europe into its field, regardless of whether Russia does become democratic. If liberal democracy does not take root in Russia, the West's policy has to concentrate more on managing Russia than on trying to reinvent it on the Western model.

East Central Europe's transition to a free-market economy and to liberal democracy is a slow and painful period, and even then it takes much longer to take roots in society than to legislate. This process suggests the need for a more nuanced approach toward the countries seeking early membership in NATO. The standard definitions of democracy—the choice of government through multiparty elections—clearly apply to the Czech Republic, Poland, and Hungary. But communism destroyed the institutional and structural framework of capitalism: private property, the rule of law, free markets for goods and services, and human rights. And liberal capitalism as democracy's groundwork is still shaky. That situation is why the most ardent reformers are seeking NATO membership so badly. They know how precarious democracy still is, as voters in many former Soviet satellites turn increasingly to governments offering socialist-style security. The reformers' intention in expanding NATO is to guarantee the results of reform so far, to improve their economic conditions, to strengthen democracy, and to create stability in the region.

While the decision to adopt relatively shaky new members will be good for Poles, Czechs, and Hungarians, it promises to weaken NATO. The more the members with different national interests, the less the ability to take rapid decisions in a complex crisis. Witness NATO's inability to act in the former Yugoslavia.

Russia's Role

Russia has fundamentally changed since the Gorbachev days. But the abandonment of the Soviet system was never the equivalent of a complete conversion to Western democratic values. A capitalist economy, the rule of law, individual rights, and other essentials of a democratic society have yet to be built in Russia. Efforts persist to restore Russia's control over the newly independent states.

Russia's Westernizers, who do not oppose NATO enlargement, correctly realizing that NATO members close to Russia's border would bring closer the zone of peace and democracy, which is in Russia's interest, are a marginal group within the elite. Nor do they have much impact on society.

The old Communist-nationalists—Lenin used to say, "Scratch a Russian Communist, and you will discover a great-Russian chauvinist"—are committed to restoring the centralized power and Russia to controlling the region once ruled by the Soviet Union.

Russia's post-Communist autocrats propose to continue what has been the messy transition to market, a limited democracy and keeping Russia together—even with force, if considered as necessary. They believe that the continuation of reforms eventually will restore Russia as a superpower.

Western indecision persuaded most of Russia's political elite that the West still considers Russia as a superpower able to veto Western decisions. Nationalists and post-Communists vigorously object to NATO enlargement, for it jeopardizes Russia's ability to influence European events. Russia's problem is not NATO membership of her Eastern neighbors. It is the denial of her status as an important participant in the emerging new Europe, which will be the result of NATO enlargement without granting Russia a special status.

Partnership for Peace was fuzzy politics, treating emerging friendly democracies the same way as a reemerging autocratic rival superpower, trying to please both without consequences for the West. By employing the tactic "negotiations to admit them," the West risks missing a historic opportunity to bring the East Central Europeans safely into the Western fold and to create a new relationship with Russia, even for the price of a weaker NATO. The overemphasis on Russia has led the alliance to neglect countries that are much more likely than Russia to become truly democratic.

If the West's priority is negotiating a security system in Europe in which Russia could play a full part, there has to be NATO enlargement, for NATO is the only functioning security framework covering the steadily integrating western part of the continent, including the increasingly westernizing former "external" empire of the Soviet Union. Partnership for Peace has proved that a special NATO-Russia relationship, at least in the field of security, is possible and necessary and that it can become an enduring framework for cooperation.

Now what is needed is real leadership. Russia remains reluctant to accept the idea that NATO will admit and protect new members. Western public opinion is reluctant to accept that Russia deserves a special status, regardless of whether she is democratic or not, for Russia remains a nuclear superpower, and no single country has a greater influence on the future of Eurasia. And potential new members do not like the idea that they have to compromise on some sensitive issues—no NATO troops on their soil, no deployment of nuclear weapons, for example, as East Germany did in 1990 to receive Gorbachev's yes for united Germany's NATO membership.

The Eurocorps: A NATO Pillar, Not Placebo

MARK P. LAGON

Senior foreign and defense policy analyst, House Republican Policy Committee, U.S. Congress

Jacques Chirac and Helmut Kohl dined in Bonn on May 10, 1996, and agreed to step up Franco-German military integration. They scheduled a bilateral summit in Dijon on June 5 to address political and military cooperation. They reported on their efforts to European Union partners at a European Council meeting June 21 and 22 and to all the advanced industrial countries in their June 27–29 summit in Lyon.

This flurry of activity in mid-1996 focused on the development of the Franco-German Eurocorps. The Eurocorps is the culminating symbol of what Harvard political scientist Karl Deutsch called the creation of a "security community" in post–World War II Europe. A *security community* is a group of nations that no longer prepare for war against one another. Late-twentieth-century amnesia obscures what an achievement it is to take Franco-German peace for granted.

The Eurocorps is a good thing for America if it sustains the European pillar of a two-pillar alliance. It is good for America if it facilitates burden sharing and some power sharing in a renegotiation of the North Atlantic Treaty Organization contract.

Yet the Eurocorps will not be a basis for a viable European security identity. In fact, nothing will. That identity will always be as ethereal as the label itself. In his *Memoirs*, the architect of the European Community, Jean Monnet, admits that "the European Defence Community project was no doubt premature." But the moment for a self-reliant European army is no more ripe than when Rene Pleven proposed the EDC in 1950.

The European security identity is nothing more than a placebo. Even Brussels Eurocrats in the Directorate of External Political Relations of the European Commission have told me that the efforts to create a common European Union foreign and defense policy are more form than substance.

On the microlevel of policy making, one can see how an independent EU defense apparatus will not work. For instance, as a function of heightened Franco-German cooperation, Jacques Chirac has been reducing the French budget deficit (matching the austerity the Federal Republic has implemented to finance the absorption of the eastern *Länder*). And one result of Chirac's shift away from his progrowth campaign rhetoric at Helmut Kohl's urging has been the strikingly un-French proposal to cut defense spending. If an EU defense is ever to work, it would have to rely on the *exporting* of France's commitment to military preparedness, not its diminution in France itself.

Moreover, the European Union utterly failed when the Bush administration foolishly ceded it responsibility for the Balkans imbroglio. The most striking legacy of those EU efforts is the unjust partition of Bosnia that David Owen proposed with Cyrus Vance and that is executed in the Dayton Accords. When the EU proposed to reward Bosnian Serb ethnic cleansing with territory won by aggression, it sought to do so openly rather than obfuscate that fact as the Clinton administration has.

The EU's failure to cope with the Bosnia problem is not a sign that a common foreign and defense policy was in an embryonic stage; it is a sign of what we can always expect from our allies if the United States washes its hands of a so-called European problem. If the Euro*corps* is designed to be the *core* of a security identity, it is bad news not just for Americans but for the Europeans themselves. A *U.S.-less* alliance would be a largely *useless* alliance.

The Imperative of U.S. Leadership

If the Eurocorps helps displace the United States from the role as leader of the caucus of the world's democracies, it will have a destructive effect. As Max Singer has argued in his book with the late Aaron Wildavsky, *The Real World Order* (1993), and elsewhere, a caucus of democracies can build peace through its own strength. Why was neoconservative icon Jean-Francois Revel so thoroughly wrong in opening *How Democracies Perish* (1983) by observing "democracy may, after all, turn out to have been a historical accident, a brief parenthesis that is closing before our eyes" ? Because American leadership overcame that inconsistent and conciliatory statecraft with which "decadent Europe"—as Revel's fellow Frenchman Raymond Aron called it—was intermittently afflicted.

U.S. leadership is still a prerequisite for the success of the democracies in coping with the less pressing but very real threats of the post–cold war order, whether applying the unique American lift capability to deliver the West's troops to fires to be extinguished or serving an ideological role as the beacon of freedom.

One class of those threats has been given the ubiquitous if unartful name *rogue nations*, as the purposeful purveyors of terrorism and weapons of mass destruction. Emphasis on the *tools* they employ—such as biological, chemical, or nuclear weapons—diverts one's attention from their anti-Western *intent*. It is intent rather than capability that makes Iran, Iraq, Libya, Syria, and North Korea dangerous. Their intent is to engage in a cheap, if disruptive, civilizational struggle for legitimacy against the West, as Samuel Huntington has rightly warned. The United States must lead the caucus of democracies in confronting these anti-Western agitators.

The Bottom-up Review—premised on preparing to fight two rogue nations—has taken Americans' focus off Russia and China. After all, these two great powers have supplied components of weapons of mass destruction and ballistic missiles to deliver them to the likes of Iran. The EU will be no more capable of confronting these two nations alone (if their leadership transitions do not evolve as we hope) than they have been willing to stand tough against the likes of Iran.

It is worth noting that both these threats, smaller radical powers as well as Russia and China, necessitate the deployment of ballistic missile defense. If the West is to pursue the common missile defense system Margaret Thatcher called for at the New Atlantic Initiative Congress of Prague, and it should, the United States will have to supply this public good.

The United States can expect support from the Eurocorps' two sponsors. The United States has long been able to count on German allegiance to its leadership role and can still do so. And Germany is the strongest European proponent of an idea the United States also must embrace: the eastward expansion of NATO's scope.

France is increasingly enthusiastic about NATO in the Chirac presidency, following a trajectory subtly but clearly set by François Mitterrand. The greatest side benefit of Clinton policy in the Balkans has not been involvement of Russian troops in Operation Joint Endeavor, as the administration claims. It has been the significant steps toward France's reintegration into the formal NATO command structure following the Dayton Accords.

Tools for the Future

The United States should take advantage of the ever-reliable Federal Republic and an increasingly cooperative France to set about two tasks in the transatlantic partnership. That partnership should renovate an old transatlantic bridge and construct a new one.

The bridge to renovate is NATO. The key task is to extend the bridge to Central Europe. The alliance should remain quietly aware that the most likely threat to European stability is still headquartered in Moscow. NATO should incorporate Poland, Hungary, the Czech Republic, and, soon, the Baltic states, to protect their newfound freedom.

Renovation requires a new bargain for burden sharing and some power sharing. The United States has long suffered from schizophrenia about European burden sharing. On the one hand, it has been eager to reduce its financial responsibility for European defense. On the other hand, it does not relish the thought of the Europeans going their own way and no longer submitting to what jargon lovers call "American hegemony." Like the conflicted parent of adolescents, the United States is eager to see the teenagers fend for themselves but wonders if they are up to the task. They are not.

The United States should not blame the EU for trying to establish a security identity. As Max Beloff chronicled in *The United States and the Unity of Europe* (1963), the United States loudly cheered on the European integration project in the first half of the cold war as a way to bolster Europe against the Soviet threat. In the second half of the cold war, the United States rightly encouraged the creation of a European pillar in the NATO alliance to achieve burden sharing.

Today, the Eurocorps can be a substantial supporting structure in a renovated NATO bridge as a basis for burden and power sharing. But the power sharing that accompanies burden sharing should be limited so that the United States remains the alliance's helmsman.

The new bridge to erect is a transatlantic free trade area (TAFTA). Instead of focusing on opening a free trade area in our hemisphere to *developing* nations, and on the as yet *"emerging"* markets of Asia, the United States should first establish a free trade area with the region where most of the advanced industrial democracies are located: Europe. A TAFTA would give the United States a greater voice in EU economic and political affairs in the aftermath of the 1996 Intergovernmental Conference. Then, for instance, American encouragement to the Europeans to first widen rather than deepen the EU would not fall on deaf ears. The United States could argue that membership in the TAFTA and the EU would do more to bolster Central European democracies in an era of ascendent, opportunistic neo-Communists than even NATO membership.

As long as the Eurocorps is not a placebo convincing the Europeans that they can defend themselves and fend for themselves, it can serve a purpose. But that purpose should be defined in terms of an overarching agenda of renovating the bridge across the Atlantic that has weathered so much in the past half century and building a commercial one alongside it.

A Wayward Child–The Growth of EU Foreign Policy and British Interests

David Matthews

Editor, European Journal

Only ten years ago, the European Community had no foreign policy. Yet at the 1996 Intergovernmental Conference (IGC), the Euro-federalists were eager to push for a full foreign and security policy and to initiate steps toward the creation of European Union armed forces. It is a long way to have traveled in a relatively short time, and the past decade has not been a success for the community's first forays into foreign policy. But for the federalists, whose ambition it is to create a new state—a United States of Europe—the creation of a foreign and defense policy is overdue. This and the single currency are the last cornerstones of the European project to be put in place.

It is true that there is already community foreign policy making of sorts, but this is not the kind that the federalists are seeking. The Single European Act of 1986 set up European Political Cooperation (EPC), which provided for cooperation between the member-states on the political and economic aspects of security policy. The EPC, however, was entirely an intergovernmental arrangement—outside the jurisdiction of community institutions—and was simply tacked on to the main body of the act, which was to create a single market. The Maastricht Treaty, signed in 1991 and ratified in 1993, set up the Common Foreign and Security Policy (CFSP). Again, its workings were meant to be intergovernmental, but member-states differed as to the significance of this. The British government described it as a "triumph" that foreign policy would avoid the clutches of the community's institutions, claiming that this heralded a new era of decentralization and a move away from federalism. Other member-states, notably Germany, and the European Commission and European Parliament regarded it as a halfway house toward full community competence. As the IGC gathers pace, the latter view is prevailing, and, not for the first time, Britain appears isolated and helpless in the face of the federalist tide. Already the British foreign secretary, Malcolm Rifkind, has agreed that someone should be appointed to represent the European Union's foreign policy.

Impact on the United States

If the federalists have their way at the IGC, the consequent treaty will create a full European Union foreign policy. This will have important consequences for the United States. American support for European integration, which has been continuous since the inception of the community, seems to be based, at least in part, on two objectives: solving the problem—once voiced by Henry Kissinger—of whom American administrations should talk to when they want to consult the Europeans as a group and having the Europeans do more to take care of the security of their continent.

These objectives, however, make the assumptions that Europeans will be able to make coherent, decisive, and long-term foreign policy and that this policy will be agreeable to the Americans. At first sight these seem reasonable assumptions. After all, aren't all the European countries democracies? Hasn't the North Atlantic Treaty Organization worked well? Don't the Europeans like to boast that the European Union has a larger gross domestic product than the United States? So what is the problem about the Europeans agreeing to positions on foreign policy and providing for their own security arrangements, which will be naturally sympathetic to the country across the Atlantic that has done so much for them this century? Like parents who hope that their offspring will have the same values and attitudes as they have and will be capable and responsible enough to lead their own lives, the Americans assume that the Europeans are finally ready to handle foreign policy on their own and will share American concerns and objectives.

But on the evidence of European foreign policy making so far, there is not much cause for optimism in Washington. The war in the former Yugoslavia demonstrated that both assumptions were wrong: European policy was neither coherent and decisive nor in agreement with American policy. When Jacques Poos, speaking for the community in 1991, declared that "now is the hour of Europe," and Jacques Delors, president of the European Commission, warned the Americans to stay out of Yugoslavia, it appeared as if the Europeans were finally growing up and handling their own back-yard problems. Five years later, such ambition seems laughable—adolescent boasting that resulted only in a mess that Uncle Sam was obliged to help clean up. Certainly, the Balkans are enough to confound the best foreign policy, but what was significant was the speed at which a common European foreign policy broke down. It took only Germany to recognize Croatia unilaterally (and prematurely, some say) to sow the seeds for the end of a clear and effective European policy and the emergence of the Contact Group, bringing in America and Russia. Given the Europeans' priority of having a common foreign policy at all costs, it was inevitable that the twisting and turning necessary to keep all the member-states on board would eventually cause the CFSP's collapse. The inadequacy of community decision making was further demonstrated when, as the State Department put it, "Europe slept" while the Americans separated the Greeks and the Turks in the Adriatic.

Changes in the Policy Mechanism

European federalists maintain that the CFSP does not work because it is outside the competence of the community's institutions and because it can make decisions only by unanimity. Hence, the federalists plan to abolish the national veto and to introduce majority voting. This, they believe, will create more efficient decision making and, with the additional input of the community's institutions—the commission, parliament, and court—will lead to clear European policy. Kissinger's problem will be solved—Washington need only call Brussels. But this disregards the fact that there is nothing more sensitive than foreign policy and national security. Allowing member-states to be outvoted on questions of vital national interest creates the conditions for the breakup of the community. The national interests of fifteen countries cannot be easily subsumed into one policy. The alternative, for the sake of keeping the community together, is to reduce foreign policy to bland, meaningless statements designed to upset no one.

The latter is Germany's favored option. It wants not only a European Union foreign and defense policy but also a pan-European security structure that would bring in the Russians. This plan, more than any other, ought to be ringing alarm bells in Washington. Russia has always wanted to be included in a common European policy to neutralize Western Europe and the American presence. It is true that Germany remains, ostensibly, a strong supporter of NATO and the Americans and that France has recently rejoined the transatlantic alliance. But their main objective for a collective European security arrangement is incompatible with NATO. Germany and France will transform NATO by building up its European component—the Western European Union (WEU), which will become the defense arm of the EU and which will, no doubt, come to an accommodation with Russia—so that its pan-European nature will make the traditional role of NATO redundant. Under such a collective system effective decision making will be impossible. As Kissinger said of the Organization for Security and Cooperation in Europe, which has more than fifty members, What have Holland and Uzbekistan got in common?[1]

At present, the British government is trying to resist the abolition of the national veto and to maintain NATO's status as the mainstay of European security. To that end, they can employ powerful arguments. The whole European political project is losing its appeal among Europeans: they are wary of the single currency; many despair of the incompetence and inefficiency of the community's current federal programs—the Common Agricultural Policy and the Common Fisheries Policy; and some are frustrated with the unaccountability of the community's institutions and their passion for bureaucracy. The public would therefore be suspicious of those same community institutions being involved in questions of national security. But as with so many areas of community policy, the likelihood is that Britain will be dragged along, reluctant to be left out and hoping, wrongly, that being a part of a common foreign policy will increase her influence. Already Britain has gone along with the idea of subsuming the WEU into the EU.

The United States should do what it can to support the British government. It is certainly not in America's interests to have European security languish under a collective Germano-Russian arrangement. Moreover, action further afield by America's traditional ally, Britain, would also be limited: there is no doubt that had a common European security policy been in place at the time of the Gulf war, Britain would not have been allowed to side with the Americans and take part. Most Europeans were extremely reluctant to get involved—the Belgians even refused to lend Britain small arms ammunition—so Britain would simply have been outvoted in the

---

1. Furthermore, undermining NATO by building up a defense arm of the EU risks alienating two of the Atlantic alliance's most important members—Turkey and Norway, neither of which is a member of the EU.

Council in Brussels and its troops would have had to stay at home. Similarly, America would no longer be able to rely on British support on the Security Council at the United Nations; in time our seat will be replaced by European Union representation.

America must prepare itself for a European foreign policy driven by the political motive of having a "national" policy at all costs. For some time, the federalists have complained that the EU's economic clout has not been matched by foreign and defense capabilities; they are eager for the EU to flex its muscles in the international arena, to prove that it is the equal of the United States, Russia, and China. There is an underlying anti-American chauvinism to much of this, a feeling of resentment and jealousy that America still holds so much sway in Europe.[2] Combine these ambitions and prejudices with a continental history of protectionism and America should begin to think of the EU as a competitor rather than a partner. At the end of a recent EU summit in Florence, the European Council issued its communiqué. It contained statements on the former Yugoslavia, the Middle East, the Mediterranean, Turkey, Chile, Uzbekistan, Asia, the Baltic states, Latin America and the Caribbean, Africa, and the World Trade Organization. Though most of the communiqué's remarks were bland, its scope should be noted. The EU is committed to a global foreign policy. But what should be noted as well is the statement,

> Notwithstanding the positive developments and the achievements in the relationship between the two sides of the Atlantic, the European Council reiterates its deep concern over the extraterritorial effects of the "Cuban Liberty and Democratic Solidarity (Libertad) Act" adopted by the United States and similar pending legislation regarding Iran/Libya. In this respect, it asserts its right and intention to react in defence of the European Union's interest in respect to this legislation and any other secondary boycott legislation having extraterritorial effects.

---

2. Recently France demanded that the head of NATO's southern flank–who is responsible for the U.S. Sixth Fleet–be replanced by a European. They also insisted that the new secretary-general of the UN should be from a Francophone country. Both these strident demands were quite easily crushed by the United States. But in the future France will not be speaking alone: it knows how to pull the strings in Brussels and will ensure that its voice will be heard through a European foreign policy. Will, then, the United States be able to get its way when faced with the whole of the EU?

In the grand scheme of foreign policy, this is not of great importance, but its significance is that such a statement would have been
unthinkable ten years earlier. In those days, the British, under Margaret Thatcher, would no doubt have been resolutely behind Washington or, at the least, have kept quiet. Now, for the sake of an easy
life, Britain goes along with a statement whose posturing should
give the Americans an inkling of what is to come.

Now that the cold war has ended and with an administration
and public more concerned with domestic problems, it is easy for
America to be complacent about European security. But unless the
United States protects NATO, the organization that has served both
Europe and America so well, and unless it supports the ability of
Britain, its chief foreign and defense policy ally, to retain its right of
independent action, the United States will find that the continent it
has done so much for in this century will in the next be paralyzed by
security arrangements that will leave America isolated and with
greatly reduced power to influence and intervene.

U.S.-European Security Relations: The Lessons of Bosnia

Joshua Muravchik
Resident scholar, American Enterprise Institute

During the latter part of the cold war, complaints were heard on
both sides of the Atlantic concerning the distribution of burdens and
authority between America and its European allies. Americans spoke
of the need for greater burden sharing, while Europeans complained
about Washington's tendency to make decisions for the alliance without adequate consultation. Under the urgencies of the cold war, little
was done to address these dissatisfactions, but when the East-West
conflict subsided, the time became ripe for a new balance in the Atlantic partnership.

The test case was Bosnia. Yugoslavia started to disintegrate in
1991, only months after the completion of Operation Desert Storm.
The American government was averse to tackling a major new secu-

rity crisis, and, conversely, many Europeans felt that the appropriate situation had arisen for a greater exercise of leadership on their own part. In June 1991, U.S. Secretary of State James Baker traveled to Belgrade to help mediate among the parties, but he stopped en route at a Berlin meeting of the Conference on Security and Cooperation in Europe, where he carefully coordinated his stance with that of the Europeans.

In Belgrade, Baker found the Yugoslav parties inflexible, and this frustration reinforced his inclination that America take a back seat in this crisis. For their part, the Europeans were ready to demonstrate their independence. Chairman of the European Community Jacques Delors put it acerbically: "We do not interfere in American affairs. We hope they will have enough respect not to interfere in ours." In July, a month after Baker's fruitless mission, a delegation of three EC foreign ministers departed for Belgrade. "This is the hour of Europe, not the hour of the Americans," declared its leader, Jacques Poos of Luxembourg.

Looking back a few years later, David Owen, who served from 1992 until 1995 as the EC representative in Yugoslav-related diplomacy, captured the push-pull dynamic between the Atlantic allies:

> There was a feeling that Europe could do it all on its own. . . .
> Europe wanted to stand on its own feet—Yugoslavia was
> the virility symbol of the Euro-federalists. This was going
> to be the time when Europe emerged with a single foreign
> policy and therefore it unwisely shut out an America only
> too happy to be shut out.

The Failure of European Policy

Rarely in the messy world of international relations does a policy notion get such a clear trial, with such clear results, as the Yugoslav crisis provided for the theory that Europe could act on its own in security matters. Yugoslavia constituted as promising a venue for such action as one could imagine. An integral part of Europe to which England, France, Germany (not to mention Austria) each felt a special tie, Yugoslavia under Communist rule had been by far the closest to the West of any Communist state. Not only did its location and history make Yugoslavia a fitting place for European action, but also its size. This was not China; this was not Ukraine; this was not even—in military capacity—Iraq. This was a small-scale crisis, when measured not in terms of human suffering but in terms of the military challenge that might have to be reckoned with.

And yet Europe proved helpless. Helpless to keep Yugoslavia intact. Helpless to prevent Belgrade from attacking Slovenia, then Croatia, then Bosnia. Helpless to prevent ethnic cleansing and even mass extermination.

Perpetual diplomatic missions of the European Union yielded nothing, but that was only the beginning of the failure. When, in May 1993, Secretary of State Warren Christopher presented to England and France President Clinton's plan to lift the arms embargo on the Bosnian government and to undertake airstrikes against the Serbs, they objected vociferously. Yielding, Washington fell in behind a European proposal to create safe havens to shelter the Bosnians—reservations for Muslims, they were called bitterly by Bosnian President Alija Izetbegovic. Yet, two years later, when Serbian forces overran two of these havens, Srebrenica and Zepa, visiting upon the male inhabitants of the former the most conspicuous mass annihilation in Europe since the Holocaust, Europe did not raise a finger.

On the contrary, the United Nations contingent stationed in Srebrenica, consisting of Dutch forces, compounded its failure to offer effective resistance to the advancing Serbs by pronouncing to the international media that the Serbian attackers had conducted themselves correctly. The Dutch forces had called for UN airstrikes against the Serbs, but these were quashed by the chief UN officer for Yugoslavia, French General Bernard Janvier. Janvier was keeping a promise he had made surreptitiously a month earlier to Bosnian Serb commander (and accused war criminal) Ratko Mladic that there would be no further Western airstrikes if the Serbs released several hundred (largely French) UN soldiers being held hostage.

True, both Janvier and the Dutch soldiers at Srebrenica were acting in the name of the UN, not of Europe. But they are Europeans. Moreover, the principal European powers insisted on preserving a major role for the UN in the Bosnian crisis, even long after UN fecklessness became manifest. They insisted on the notorious dual key, which allowed UN General Secretary Boutros Boutros-Ghali and his representatives to block the North Atlantic Treaty Organization's airstrikes time and again. Apparently, this was precisely the reason they wished to give him such authority.

Moreover, the Europeans also staunchly resisted the lifting of the UN's arms embargo on Bosnia. And they threatened to with-

147

draw their contingents of UN forces in the event that the United States broke the embargo. Yet, they also made clear that they felt incapable of extricating their own forces: they let it be known that they would look to American assistance in any such operation. That is, the Europeans could not even take an action designed to protest American policy without American help. In the end, this may have been all to the good because the threat of having to send troops to Bosnia to extricate allied forces roused Washington from its inertia.

Catalyst of U.S. Leadership

The result was the Dayton Accords. History is not likely to judge these a success. Nonetheless, they represented a step forward from the pathetic paralysis of Western policy exhibited over the preceding three years. And they illustrated that for Europe to act—even in matters of European security—the essential ingredient is American leadership. When such leadership is supplied, the Europeans are both willing and able to pull their weight. The multinational force that interposed itself successfully between the warring Bosnian factions included as many British and French troops as Americans, with smaller numbers from many other countries. Their role was essential: the American public almost certainly would not have allowed Washington to send its sons and daughters all alone. But until Washington stepped to the front, nothing constructive happened.

Why is this so? First, while Europe may soon have a single currency, it is a long way from being a single society or polity. It is rarely of one mind about political or security challenges. In the case of Yugoslavia, Britain and France and especially Greece sympathized with the Serbs while Germany and Austria identified with the Slovenes and Croats and to a lesser degree with the Bosnians, who, in turn, enjoyed the strong sympathy of Turkey. The EU's December 1991 decision to encourage the secession of the Yugoslav republics without offering any meaningful help in keeping peace among them was the kind of incoherent, common-denominator policy that often results from a leaderless collectivity.

Second, in the political and security realm, Europe suffers from severe structural anomalies that are likely to endure for as long as memories of the two world wars are fresh. Germany is the continent's dominant economic power and, within a narrowly European context, would be the natural leader. But the history of German aggression precludes that role. In the face of the Yugoslav crisis, Germany exercised unprecedented leadership within the EU, but when the political decisions that Germany championed required backing with military muscle, Germany was helpless to act.

Third, ever since Europe came asunder so tragically and inexplicably in 1914, it has failed to rediscover the will, purpose, and political clarity needed to safeguard its own security. Between the two wars, part of Europe succumbed to tyranny while the part that remained democratic was beset by cowardice and indecision. After the second war, only American intervention protected the western part of the continent from being swallowed into the Soviet empire.

Finally, the realities of power make it exceedingly difficult for any other state to exercise leadership from within America's giant shadow. America's economic and military might (and also its mechanical and cultural inventiveness) loom so large, it is natural that in any international crisis, the other states, especially those who are America's allies, will look first to see what Washington intends to do.

Over the past half-century, the states of Western Europe performed prodigies of reconstruction, building prosperous stable democracies on the ashes of wartime destruction. Since 1989, Central Europeans have begun to mirror this achievement. But in the realm of security, the sad experience of Bosnia demonstrated powerfully that Europe remains dependent on leadership from America.

Is There a Perception of a Common Threat?

RICHARD ROSE
Director, Centre for the Study of Public Policy

Common defense requires the perception of a common threat; only then are people willing to pool resources and risks under the leadership of the strongest power or powers. This explains the creation of the North Atlantic Treaty Organization in 1949. The free nations of Europe were immediately threatened by the Soviet Union; the United States saw a Soviet takeover in Europe as a threat to American interests, too; and America was the only country with the military might capable of deterring Soviet expansion.

But in the past decade, there have been fundamental shifts in world politics. The fall of the Berlin Wall has moved the boundaries of free Europe to the Baltic and the Black Sea. The Soviet Union has collapsed, and weaknesses of the former Soviet Union are exposed in the battleground and black markets of Chechnya. Europeans have been making common cause politically and economically. To most Europeans, Brussels now symbolizes the headquarters of the expanding fifteen-member European Union rather than the headquarters of NATO.

The United States has concurrently tilted toward the Pacific and Latin America: California is now the largest state in the Union. The North/South axis has gained importance in the Western Hemisphere, as the North Atlantic Free Trade Area demonstrates, and Texas and Florida are gaining importance vis-à-vis New York. In this new world, what concerns people in Warsaw may not bother people in Walla Walla, the concerns of Tampere in Finland are not those of Tampa, and the defense of Paris, France, is not the same as that of Paris, Illinois.

New Concerns

A sustainable policy for European-American relations must be based on a recognition of common interests in the world as it now is and as it is becoming. Without common interests, there is no basis for common defense or economic collaboration. Who are we?

In a democracy, a sustainable policy for defense must also be based upon popular support. It is no good for European leaders to make strategic commitments involving domestic political risks as well as risks abroad if they do not have popular backing. The aftermath of the Maastricht Treaty, in which elites entered into commitments that their national electorates have doubts about, makes European politicians gun-shy in the political as well as the military sense today. The same syndrome is evident at both ends of Pennsylvania Avenue.

Fortunately, public opinion can be measured by the familiar methods of a sample survey, and this is true in the frontline states of post-Communist Europe as well as in NATO countries. Before we take at face value claims that NATO must (or must not) be expanded eastward, it is appropriate to see what people who have spent most of their lives behind the iron curtain see as threats to their peace and security today. The evidence can be found in the autumn 1995 New

Democracies Barometer (NDB) survey of the Paul Lazarsfeld Society, Vienna, which took nationwide representative samples of more than one thousand people each in six Central and East European countries—the Czech Republic, Slovakia, Slovenia, Hungary, Poland, Bulgaria, and Romania—and in the parallel fifth New Russia Barometer, a nationwide Russian survey of more than two thousand respondents, conducted in January 1996, immediately after the Duma election.

The good news is that World War III is out of the question. The NDB survey found little fear of the United States: only 3 percent on average see America as a big threat to their national security, and another 7 percent as some threat. Germany is also usually not perceived as a threat: only 7 percent on average of Central and East Europeans see Germany as a big threat, and an additional 18 percent see it as offering some threat. Russia remains the most threatening country: 42 percent on average see some or a big threat coming from the remains of the old Soviet behemoth.

The bad news, however, is that the Balkan Wars may be back. An average of 30 percent see neighboring countries as a significant threat to peace and security, and 26 percent see national minorities within their own country as threats. The political geography means that in some instances neighboring countries can be threats to European peace as well as national peace: perceptions of threats therefore differ from country to country (see table 1).

Public opinion in Poland and the Czech Republic shows a classic concern with Great-Power conflict, for more than half the people in each country see Russia as a threat to their security, and almost half see Germany as a threat. In both cases, Germany is an immediate neighbor, and the presence of Soviet troops for two generations was a reminder that Moscow is also not distant.

By contrast, Bulgaria, Hungary, and Slovenia display characteristic Balkan concerns: neighbors and national minorities are seen as enemies. In Bulgaria, Turks are a national minority, and Turkey is a large and immediate neighbor. Hungarians constitute national minorities in three neighboring countries of a state that contracted after the downfall of the Austro-Hungarian empire: there are substantial minorities in Romania, Slovakia, and parts of Croatia. In Slovenia, the question about threats from neighbors was not asked—nor does it need to be, given that Slovenia is the one former Yugoslav republic to have extricated itself from the consequences of the violent breakup of that state. The Washington approach to Bosnia sug-

TABLE 1
PERCEIVED THREATS TO PEACE AND SECURITY

	Russia	Germany	United States	Neighbors	Own minorities
	Percent Seeing Threat to Country's Peace and Security				
Big power security needs					
Poland	70	44	7	15	8
Czech Republic	54	43	15	14	14
Neighbors as enemies					
Bulgaria	5	2	8	29	36
Hungary	29	4	4	47	14
Slovenia	21	5	4	n.a.	20
Double anxieties					
Romania	52	15	13	34	33
Slovakia	50	31	23	37	50

n.a. = not available.
SOURCE: Paul Lazarsfeld Society, Vienna, *New Democracies Barometer* 4 (autumn 1995), nationwide representative sample surveys with face-to-face interviews with 7,441 respondents.

gests that the White House and Congress are not going to station American troops permanently on the boundaries of Slovenia and Croatia. The problems of Greek-Turkish relations are a reminder that the expansion of NATO would hardly contribute to resolving frictions between Bulgaria and Turkey.

The public is doubly anxious in Romania, fearful of a Hungarian minority as well as Russia, and in Slovakia of Germany, Russia, and a Hungarian minority. Even though these countries are anxious about Russia, their eastward boundaries are with Ukraine and Moldova, not the Russian Federation, which reduces their significance as front-line countries—and their local problems are Balkan in the pejorative sense, a disincentive for American involvement.

Russians too are doubly anxious, and in keeping with the great power status of the former Soviet Union their anxieties are global in extent. The fifth New Russia Barometer survey found that in 1996 the biggest threats to Russian peace and security were seen as:

FIGURE 1
RUSSIANS' PERCEPTIONS OF EXTERNAL THREATS
TO THEIR PEACE AND SECURITY
(percent)

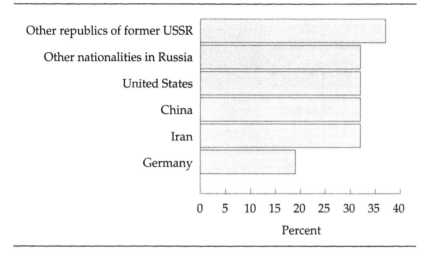

SOURCE: Adapted from Centre for the Study of Public Policy, University of Strathclyde, Glasgow, *New Russia Barometer* 5 (January 1996), face-to-face interviews with a nationwide representative sample of 2,340 persons.

Other republics of former USSR	37 percent
Other nationalities in Russia	33 percent
USA	32 percent
China	32 percent
Iran	32 percent
Germany	16 percent

New Russia Barometer surveys make clear that Belarus, Ukraine, and the Central Asian republics worry Russians; they do not feel threatened by invasion from Lithuania or conditions in Latvia and Estonia. When their minds turn outward, Russians are as likely to see threats coming from China in the east or Iran in the south as from the United States. Germany, a historical enemy and critical in NATO expansion, is least likely to be seen as a threat (figure 1).

Public opinion favors action—but not military moves of the sort that have led to Russia's first televised war in the streets of Grozny and the mountains of Chechnya (figure 2). Negotiation is unanimously endorsed. Two-thirds also favor the use of economic pres-

153

FIGURE 2
STRATEGIES PREFERRED BY RUSSIANS FOR DEALING WITH EXTERNAL THREATS
(percent)

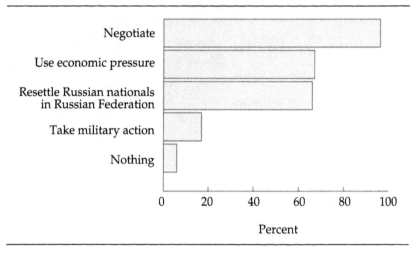

SOURCE: Adapted from Centre for the Study of Public Policy, University of Strathclyde, Glasgow, *New Russia Barometer* 4 (March–April 1995), face-to-face interviews with a nationwide representative sample of 1,943 persons.

sures, a strong card in Russian hands. If economic sanctions do not work, only one in six endorses the use of force. By contrast, two-thirds think it would be reasonable to bring Russians back home from the newly independent states, a repatriation process similar to that in Britain and in France after the end of their empires.

The existence of substantial anxieties about Russia and a widespread desire for collective defense with and against Germans indicate support for the view of State Department spokesperson Nicholas Burns when he said, "The US considers itself to be a European power" (*Financial Times*, June 4, 1996). The United States remains the biggest credible check on Russian expansion and the strongest force binding Germany to a nonthreatening alliance. It can also play an important role in reducing the threats to life across Eastern Europe from accidents at civil nuclear energy stations in the former Soviet Union.

A Different U.S. Role

But anxieties about Balkan-type troubles are a reminder that many Europeans have defense concerns that are not shared with Washington. Border difficulties along the Danube cannot be met with atomic weapons, for they would bring death to civilians as well as military on all sides of a conflagration. Balkan wars require action on the ground and often engage irregular military forces that can only be dealt with through close contact and may "dissolve" into hostile ground rather than surrender.

The bottom line is that the United States no longer wants to be or needs to be the only power in Europe. It no longer wants to be since American opinion does not define each local difficulty as a threat to global peace. Nor does it need to be when European countries have sufficient military force to deal with problems that involve a few million people at most.

Steps to differentiate NATO commitments from European commitments are to be welcomed. The Berlin meeting of NATO foreign ministers in June 1996 approved a separate role for troops now part of NATO in Balkan-style operations under the leadership of the Western European Union. While this brought France into partnership, it leaves open the position of European Union countries that are not members of NATO and have significant security concerns, such as Finland and Austria. It also leaves open questions of what can be done to mobilize national forces in countries that see their neighbors and not Moscow as a clear and present danger.

The first priority of NATO should not be expansion but rethinking, to be clear about what it is and is not designed to do in the new Europe. This is good news for Americans who want to be let off the hook of getting bogged down in the Balkans and for Europeans who do not want their own security threatened by the American presidential calendar or candidates making remarks that turn out to be more sound-bites than having real teeth when push comes to shove in the Baltic or the Balkans. When rethinking arrives at a stable understanding of responsibilities for peacekeeping, both Americans and Europeans can welcome what was implicit in Nicholas Burns's remark: today, the United States is *a* European power, not *the* European power.

Single-Market Crime: A European View

Ernesto U. Savona

Director, Research Group on Transnational Crime,
School of Law, University of Trento

The completion of the European Community's internal market on January 1, 1993, represents a historic result of the convergence of economic and political interests in one of the most developed regions in the world. The process of integration of these interests and therefore of the single policies is still continuing, but it has been progressively overshadowed, along with other economic problems such as recession or the Maastricht parameters, by the increasing rates in organized crime and terrorist activities as well as by the use of the economic and financial systems for money-laundering purposes.

Dangers from a Lack of Borders

The spirit of liberalization and openness behind the single-market program has been replaced by an increased awareness of the dangers of an interstate global crime threat and a more recent and renewed terrorist activity. Within the community, in fact, the focus is now not so much on the advantages of the abolition of border controls as on the dangers that freedom of movement represents for European security when it is not accompanied by a corresponding coordination of policies and free circulation of instruments to protect the region.

In addition to the new opportunities that have opened up for legitimate entrepreneurs, opportunities for illicit enterprises have increased. Since the crime industry is about the criminal exploitation of business opportunities, it is not surprising that we have seen the development of organizations that transport illicit commodities across national borders of one of the most important demand markets for forbidden goods.

Among the activities that criminal organizations (be they drug traffickers or terrorists) typically engage in and that will deserve further attention in the near future, drug trafficking still remains the most important source of income, but the trafficking in strategic material is a rising concern among national authorities.

This current expansion of criminal activities leads one to assume an expansion of the demand for money laundering. There is clear evidence emerging from cases in almost all European Union countries that criminals do not limit their activities to crime, but that they also exert a dangerous influence within legal markets. Europe, in fact, because of its central geopolitical position and its economic and financial markets, provides a good entry point into international legal markets. Almost all EU countries are aware of illicit capital entering their markets. In investing their surplus money, criminal organizations increasingly tend to use professionals and lawyers who can conceal the real ownership of money, thus averting the risk of its detection and seizure.

In the area of transnational crime and terrorism, what is the central problem or central threat in the foreseeable future? The European Union can be seen as the crossroads of many criminal groups operating both locally and internationally. An analysis of their activities shows a progressive emphasis on Europe and the distribution of trafficking routes either by sea, air, or land from key points of Europe to other continents.

Spain, Italy, and Portugal are still the major entry points for cocaine to Europe. Spain and Portugal, however, are increasing in importance as entry points for heroin coming from South Asia and Pakistan, via Africa (touching, among others, Angola, Mozambique, and Cape Vert). Cocaine and heroin from Spain spread into Europe through France or by sea through Italy. In both cases the Italian Mafia plays a leading role in controlling the deliveries.

Transhipment of heroin, coming from Central Asia and the Middle East, and cocaine, coming from South America, are also conducted by Nigerians via air through the main international airline points. Turks and Kurds are also involved in heroin trafficking from the production points to Germany and the United Kingdom, passing through the Balkans and Greece. Heroin distribution inside these European countries is carried out by specialized Turkish networks within their immigrant communities.

Ports and airports in Europe are the main points of distribution inside and outside Europe. Frequent examples show Nigerian criminals, specifically active in this context, as importers of cocaine and heroin along routes involving Lagos, London, Athens, Antwerp, and other main international airline points. They also act as exporters to the United States (Chicago) and Canada (Toronto). Part of the heroin imported by Nigerians and the hashish coming from Southeast Asia and Northern Africa first crosses France, then is reexported toward other European and North American markets. Opium also enters through the French borders, and after it is refined locally, it is exported as pure heroin.

The entry of eastern organized crime in the international market has changed and increased the routes traditionally used. Russia and the other Eastern European regions are increasingly becoming the new transit routes for this drug trafficking as well as for other criminal purposes, such as car theft, human smuggling, and recently strategic material trafficking. The increasing interest of criminals in strategic materials, especially nuclear materials, since the collapse of the former Soviet Union has caused considerable alarm. Although there are questions about whether there is actually a criminal or terrorist organization beyond the supply side, if they cannot find purchasers for the material in hand, then they may find extortion particularly attractive. Moreover, as nuclear disarmament continues, the availability of material is likely to increase rather than decrease. There are, in Russia, currently several hundred tons of weapon-usable fissionable material under inadequate physical security and material control. Kilogram quantities of weapon-usable fissionable materials have been stolen from institutes in Russia since the breakup of the Soviet Union. These quantities are sufficient to make small nuclear weapons. It is reasonable to conclude that sufficient fissionable material can be diverted from Russian stockpiles to provide a subnational group with one or two nuclear weapons or even a rogue state with a sizable arsenal. European countries have no real overview of how black-market plutonium is circulating but are deeply concerned about the growing evidence that Europe is becoming the main smuggling route for nuclear material from the former Soviet Union to underdeveloped states and terrorist groups.

In this context, links are increasing between criminal and terrorist groups and other external actors with organizational forms. For example, former agents of the STASI, the former East German secret police, are believed to have been instrumental in trying to establish links with their erstwhile KGB colleagues. Furthermore, the distinction between criminal organizations pursuing economic goals and terrorist groups pursuing essentially political objectives is likely to become increasingly blurred, but the threat remains equally great that the first will corrupt and exploit and the second will disrupt and destroy and use the same legal linkages to provide their resources.

Implications for the United States

Recent stringent anti–money-laundering policies and legislation adopted by the member-states have stimulated a more efficient detection of the real owners of these proceeds, the seizure of capital of illicit origin, and, in general, a more efficient common response from European law enforcement. The adoption of such measures, as well as the active participation of the EU in other international efforts and organizations aimed at countering organized crime and terrorism and the establishment of a European Police Office (Europol) to facilitate information exchange on these matters with other overseas countries (in first line with the United States), reflects general concern of the European Community about the spread of organized crime and its increasing willingness in constructing a network of international technical and legislative instruments for cooperation with other regional areas.

The implications for the Americans are therefore numerous and will develop even more in the long term, as the approach to the problem needs to be as global as the problem is. The strategies to be adopted will consist of three main steps. First, international organizations such as the Organization for Economic Cooperation and Development or the United Nations and their instruments will help regional areas establish policies for the domestic implementation of the minimum instruments. Once these have been determined, the second step is for the regions to act with the individual countries to persuade them to adopt the minimum standards of cooperation in their legislation and practice. Regional bodies, such as the European Union and the Organization of American States, as well as the countries that are part of the European Economic Area or that have signed European Economic Agreements are an essential part of this process, on which the outcome of the challenge depends, as they can take into account the countries' geographical, political, and legal peculiarities. After this step, the third step will be to move toward more uniformity among regions and therefore to evaluate further steps to counter what has been called the new world global enemy.

European Defense and European Security: And Never the Twain Shall Meet?

JAMES SHERR
Lecturer, Lincoln College, Oxford University

Even before the Berlin Wall came down in 1989, several European countries—not only a post-Gaullist France—believed that Europe should possess the means to define and act on security interests on its own, or at least be able to act on common Western security interests in its own fashion. To ask where common foreign and security policy ended and common security and defense policy began was like asking how long is a piece of string? Anyone serious about either pursuit swiftly recognized that, in a still unpredictable if no longer threatening world, security policy would carry little weight unless backed by defense capability.

Given the means required to realize the end, skeptics, including much of the British foreign policy establishment, asked two nettlesome questions: If a European defense identity was required in the interests of the European Union, was it also required in the interests of European defense? And if so, was it achievable at a cost that the members of this union would be willing to bear?

These questions have not lost their importance, but for two reasons they are no longer at the center of discussion. The first reason is the war in the former Yugoslavia: a war that not only exposed, in vindication of Euro-skeptics, the hollowness of Europe's pretension but, in vindication of Europe's advocates, the impulsiveness of U.S. policy and the power that the United States can bring to bear even when its policy is most questionable. For the United states bombed not only Bosnia's Serbs into signing the Dayton Accords but also its European allies into accepting them, despite the latter's belief that the resurrection of a multicultural Bosnia was no longer achievable and despite their conviction that there would be no long-term peace of any kind without the kind of long-term commitment that the U.S. policy rules out. Thanks to its own fecklessness, Europe has been handed a "peace" in Bosnia that it did not devise and which it seems destined to lose.

The second reason is the implications for Europe of the revival of Great Power ideology in Russia: a revival that has occurred within

160

the Yeltsin regime rather than in opposition to it and that, despite the euphoria of the moment, is likely to gather pace now that a number of hard liners and former opponents have been brought within the fold. While not intended to renew threats against the West, the "struggle for spheres of interest" to which Boris Yeltsin persistently refers has raised apprehensions in the former Warsaw Pact countries of Central Europe, not to say Ukraine, where Russian pressure is likely to become more subtle and systematic now that the election crisis is over.

It is in Germany where the determination to reconcile security in Central Europe and partnership with Russia is greatest, for it is Germany that will be affected most significantly if the Central and Eastern European status quo unravels. This prospect, slim as it might be, is already having one profound effect: the revival of Germany's anxiety about itself. If integration cannot create stability—either because it *cannot* create it or because integration itself is thwarted—will stability then have to be maintained by traditional methods? If Europe fails to act on its common interests, might Germany then have to assert its own national interests? These are disturbing questions for a country whose long-term aim has been to delegitimize not only its own national interests but also those of others.

It would be astounding if these German anxieties did not instill apprehension in France about the relevance, not to say the durability, of the German-Franco relationship: a relationship that, it is fair to say, has been inspired largely by a fear of Germany. German unification has exposed not only the limits of this relationship—and the weakness of France—but also the depth of French schizophrenia about the future of Europe. For it is axiomatic in France, as it is in Germany itself, that European integration is a mechanism for integrating Germany and keeping it locked in to Western institutions. But if this formula was adequate to managing a divided Germany constrained by the balance of terror, it does not stand to reason that a more vigorous application of it will manage a united Germany whose center of gravity, not to say economic power, has moved eastward. If "Europe" moves east to retain its influence over Germany, could the EU not find itself becoming the vehicle of German influence? If Europe acquires the attributes of supranationality—that is, a common currency well as a common defense—then who exactly will be integrating whom?

Far from reexamining the complex logic of its policy, France has devised a counterlogic alongside it: renewing its interest in the United

States as a counterweight to Germany, cultivating Britain as Europe's most Atlanticist member, and, most spectacularly of all, returning to the fold of the North Atlantic Treaty Organization. The latter development is most evident in Bosnia, where for the first time since 1966 French forces are serving under an integrated NATO command. Encouraging all of this might be. Yet the magnetic fields generated by the complexities of Franco-German policies are not only producing disorientation in Western Europe but also unsettling the relationship between European defense and European security.

Joining the West

For the reality is that a core group of Central European states is now determined, if not desperate, to join NATO. Despite their interest in European structures, and in the unique potential of the Western European Union to advance EU and NATO membership simultaneously, few people of consequence in Poland, Hungary, or the Czech Republic would dispute the British prime minister's view that "NATO and the American presence in Europe remain the bedrock of our common security."

This said, security is not the main reason that most Central European countries seek NATO membership. Rather, they are convinced that, by joining NATO, they will simultaneously join the West—a highly debatable conviction given the fact that NATO's first post–cold war applicant, Albania, and several others possess few Western attributes, that several of the most Western countries in Europe are outside NATO, and that "Westerization" has never been a large part of NATO's purpose. With greater wisdom Poland, Hungary, and the Czech Republic have an additional conviction: that NATO membership is needed to eliminate the ghosts of the *cordon sanitaire* and an aggressive Germany. Naturally, the latter quest is supported by a newly united Germany anxious to destigmatize itself as it becomes more involved in Central Europe's affairs.

The catch is that despite its overwhelming West-West rationale, NATO enlargement could create a fresh round of security problems in the East. Had events conspired to produce a post–Communist Soviet Union in 1991, these problems, and a power vacuum in Central Europe, might have existed already. Yet, today, there is no Soviet Union, only Russia, and no power vacuum in Central Europe, only a vacuum of confidence. For this reason, while the overriding political aim of Poland, the Czech Republic, and Hungary might be NATO membership, their overriding *strategic* aim must be to prevent the reconstruction of a Soviet or Russian Empire. Ukrainians are not the only people to appreciate that NATO enlargement might add to Russia's incentives to reconstitute it. Ironically, it is only by resubordinating Ukraine or the Baltic states that Russia could once again become the dominant factor in Central Europe.

The United States, as ever professing the religion of good intentions, has tried to square this circle through Partnership for Peace: like the Marshall Plan of old, open to all, but, unlike the Marshall Plan, acceded to by Russia and by thirteen other former Soviet republics. Despite the symbolic insult of placing Poland on the same formal footing as Kazakhstan, the PFP has a practical advantage for Central Europe. As a series of "sixteen-plus-one" programs, it gives individual countries the option of becoming closely associated with NATO or maintaining a purely decorative relationship.

Nevertheless, even for countries in the former group, PFP poses several practical problems. The most serious of these is that preoccupation with achieving partnership goals—interoperability, standardization, transparency in budgeting, and cooperation in peacekeeping—has diverted attention from the primary tasks of national defense: how to devise roles and operational concepts—not to say finance, equipment, and manpower—for national armed forces. While every NATO member has to confront these questions, partnership countries, accustomed to a Warsaw Pact structure, have the illusion that PFP and NATO will provide the answers. Yet PFP is simply a program for transforming the "relationship between NATO and participating states." It was never meant to provide them.

A second problem is that the participation of Central (and many Southern) European states in the United Nations Protection Force (UNPROFOR) and Implementation Force (IFOR) in Bosnia, which these participants all hope will accelerate the process of NATO enlargement, might in fact derail it. This is simply because, to its architects, IFOR is also a successful, not to say vital, exercise in the NATO-*Russian* partnership: a partnership that, in the Balkans and elsewhere, could well be threatened if NATO moves east. Thus, the risk of a crisis in Eastern Europe is not unthinkable.

Had Europe been able to transcend its own introversion even two years ago—and the Clinton administration been able to see beyond its own platitudes—these risks might have been made much smaller than they are today. Since the end of the cold war, NATO and the EU have faced the same fundamental challenge: to advance the substance, rather than the symbols, of integration and security in Central Europe and to do so in a way that does not transform new members of the West into front-line states. To this end, we would have been well advised to exploit the *deterrent* potential of enlargement, undertaking not to move east unless Russia moved west. Such a policy would have required us to understand that a NATO retaining its military seriousness could not enlarge without risk of provoking or endangering those that enlargement excluded. Such a policy would have required a geopolitical approach to security that post–cold war orthodoxies rule out.

In 1997, after years of pandering to the orthodoxies rather than the realities of the post–cold war era, the reversal of policy on enlargement not only would undermine Western credibility but also could produce despair in Central Europe and possibly its "loss." Given our collective failures to date, there are probably no good policies left. It remains to be seen whether we will at least summon the will to achieve lesser evils.

Central Europe and NATO

RADEK SIKORSKI
Author, former deputy defense minister of Poland

Seven years after the collapse of communism and five years since we knocked at NATO's door for the first time, I believe that both Central Europe and the West have missed important opportunities.

In 1989, as Communist regimes crashed one by one, the West enjoyed a unique moral as well as political and economic preeminence. Perhaps naively, those of us who had identified with the struggle for democracy and capitalism against oppression believed that the West could do virtually no wrong. The example of leaders such as Ronald Reagan and Margaret Thatcher (who was still in power at the time) inspired us to believe in the community of Western values, a community to which, by virtue of our long and hard struggle against the common foe, we felt we belonged by right and would soon belong by law.

But many things that have happened in the world since 1989 have blunted our enthusiasm. The following immediately spring to mind:

- George Bush encouraged Iraqi Shiites to rise up against Saddam Hussein and then failed to help them.
- During three years of slaughter, Western powers kept telling the Bosnians that they must not be supplied with weapons to defend themselves because this would "only prolong their suffering."
- Western security guarantees to defend the United Nations "safe zones" of Srebrenica, Zepa, and Gorazde were broken.
- The brutal war in Chechnya met with muted Western criticism: billions of dollars of Western funds continue to prop up the Russian government even while Russians export capital and while Russia prosecutes the war. Russia's breaking of the Conference on Security and Cooperation in Europe rules on the movement of troops went unremarked. Instead, despite failing standards on many counts, Russia has been admitted into the Council of Europe.
- The Conventional Forces in Europe Treaty on conventional arms, broken in Chechnya, was amended to suit the needs of Russia's ambitions in the Caucasus.

These disparate events add up to a pattern of strategic muddle, lack of statesmanship, and faithlessness. Such Western behavior is particularly worrying for Central Europe, which has always been peripheral to Western interests. Countries such as Poland and the Czech Republic can be forgiven for believing that if the West is capable of breaking a security guarantee to one faraway place, it may well fail to honor a solemn treaty to aid another.

Hence, the romantic phase of our infatuation with the West has given way to a more sober view of the West's true intentions and capabilities in the region. We now know what we did not know five years before: that any security treaty with the West may or may not be honored depending on the circumstances. If push comes to shove, we can probably count only on ourselves.

Fortunately, the urgency of seeking alliances against a resurgence of Russian aggression in Central Europe has lessened. Russia has proved in Chechnya that its army is in a state of near collapse. Its equipment as well as stocks of spares, ammunition, and food has deteriorated, and the Russian army is unlikely to be able to carry out a major offensive war anytime soon. Drafting the entire nation into the ranks and using irregular tactics on our own territory, Poland on its own could probably fight a Russian invasion to a standstill much the way Finland did in 1939–1940.

Such a scenario is, of course, extremely unlikely at present. Of more practical concern for us is the question of how to react to Russian attempts to regain dominance over the territory of the former Soviet Union, particularly Ukraine. As the historian Norman Davies has argued, Russia plus Ukraine equals the Russian Empire. Whenever Russia managed to take control of Ukraine in the past, Poland was next in line for subjugation. If Poland were to choose to enter the North Atlantic Treaty Organization at the price of allowing Ukraine to fall under Russian control or be left out of NATO but with Ukraine continuing as an independent country, it should choose the latter. The pressure on Ukraine is unlikely to be military. We can best maintain Ukraine as a friendly buffer and start tying it to the West by extending to it major European road, railway, and power networks and by shoring up the Ukrainian economy through free trade.

But the realization that we are largely on our own means that Central European powers will be more hardheaded in their dealings with the West. This approach can already be seen in Poland's relations with the European Union. In 1990, we unilaterally lifted most tariffs and stared in stupefied incomprehension when the European Union failed to respond in kind. Today, when Brussels complains of Polish tariffs on its goods, Polish officials coolly point out that the union continues to run a large trade surplus with Poland and that tariff reductions can be handled in negotiations on our full membership in the union. The same is likely to happen in our dealings with NATO. Five years ago, we jumped at every alliance suggestion. Today, we will treat the offer of NATO membership as serious only if it contains material assurances of the West's good faith, such as the stationing of Western tripwire forces on our territory.

NATO Enlargement: America's Stake in European Stability

EDWARD STREATOR

Chairman, The New Atlantic Initiative, and former U.S. ambassador, Organization for Economic Cooperation and Development

As a contribution to stability in Europe—the source of two world conflicts and still a danger to American security interests—the United States should press for the admission of Poland, the Czech Republic, and Hungary to full membership in the North Atlantic Treaty Organization by the year 2000. After protracted temporizing, a serious debate at last is being joined in the United States and other allied countries on the question of admitting new members to NATO. The resolution of this issue, and its timing, will determine to a great extent the future orientation of the alliance, the degree of public support it enjoys, and perhaps its continued existence in the post-Communist era. Uncertainties arising from failure to resolve this question sooner have already handicapped progress in shaping positively the evolution of policies of the vital treaty partnership that has been the guarantor of Western security during almost half a century. For most, including the United States and governments of other NATO members, the answer is clear: NATO enlargement's advantages far outweigh the disadvantages. But a vocal minority of strategic thinkers on both sides of the Atlantic believes the opposite. Analysis of the contrary arguments, however, shows them lacking in decisive weight.

Those favoring the status quo advance strategic and political arguments assuming that the current and likely evolution of security in Europe and elsewhere does not require adjustments for adequate deterrence and defense. They also assume that such adjustments would only impair a natural emergence of a new European continental order finally free of the conflicts that have cost millions of lives over centuries. This line of thought ignores the lesson finally learned only in this century: cooperative international endeavor that is active and geared to the times deters and deals better with aggression than Micawberesque passivity.

From a military viewpoint, some argue that NATO needs no overhaul, because no serious threat to Western security exists after the crippling of the formerly formidable Soviet war machine by the dissolution of the Soviet Union. Others argue that clever Russian Federation leaders have now learned that there never was a Western threat to the Soviet Union. These arguments overlook, however, the nuclear arsenals still at the disposal of the states of the former Soviet Union and discount the malignant nationalism that lies just beneath the surface of contemporary politics there. Moreover, they seem to take for granted the unperturbed evolution of the federation states into paragons of stability abjuring rapacity.

Contemporary Risks

Today's uncertain temper of the federation states belies such optimism, however, and the risks are palpable there of ethnic-based and other conflicts, with attendant possibilities of wider conflagrations threatening more horrors like those in the former Yugoslavia, which tied the West in knots literally for years. At worst, such conflicts, by inviting intervention, could ignite continental instability. At best, they would challenge the NATO allies seeking to damp the fires in the interests of human rights even if no other interests were threatened.

Enlarging NATO by including at least Poland, the Czech Republic, and Hungary will help to offset these dangers by underlining to allied publics and to potential adversaries the firm intention of the West to preserve and enhance NATO's political and security instruments allowing positive allied engagement in the event of need and based on allied consensus. The dynamic of enlargement, supported by the United States, also will dramatize to the American public the continuing relevance of the NATO alliance and thus help ensure the continued commitment of the United States and its massive deterrent capabilities to the defense of Europe and U.S. interests there, at a time when isolationist pressures in the United States are threatening to undermine support for the security dispositions that characterized the cold war.

Enlargement will also associate key Central and Eastern European states in the network of associations in and parallel to NATO. This would help attenuate tendencies to internal conflict within the new member-states, and also help to insulate these former Soviet satellites from intimidation by a resurgent Russia and from possible spillovers of conflicts arising to the East. Moreover, inclusion of the new members in the NATO family will make easier the kind of palliative involvement in interallied relations that has characterized NATO's role in easing tensions in the relationships between Greece and Turkey, which, while members of the alliance, harbor deep, historic mutual antagonisms.

In short, NATO membership will broaden and deepen the circle of stability at Europe's center, with the political and economic benefits that confident association in the alliance on a permanent and defined basis would allow.

Some argue that NATO expansion will not allow time for new democratic institutions to become embedded in the Russian Federation before throwing down a challenge that would incur serious Russian displeasure or worse when its more liberal leaders are seeking to build democracy with fragile support already endangered by military and other nationalistic opponents. Some also assert that NATO expansion, by shifting NATO's national perimeters eastward, will stall efforts to build on constructive relations between the federation states and the West in such matters as arms control and disarmament. There is little doubt that opponents of NATO enlargement are a powerful element in Russian ruling circles. Yet, there has never been from the Russian side the kind of firm rejection that would suggest a uniform view of its implications among the Russian leadership. It is also true that the West has trod gingerly, and none more than the Clinton administration, with its temporizing Partnership for Peace initiative, which served a limited but perhaps useful purpose. Thus, the Russians have not been impelled to take a firm stand and may actually see bargaining leverage in being led to grudging acquiescence.

But it is equally clear that further equivocation will not serve the West's interests. It will embolden the Russians to believe they might or intimidate the allies on the issue of enlargement. More important, perhaps, it will deeply discourage the applicants themselves, which are committed to democracy and solidarity with the allies and which seek recognition as equal partners in the search for a more stable order in Europe. Rejection would damage the standing of the current liberal leaders of the Eastern and Central European states and encourage the emergence of other, more nationalistic leaders espousing alternative ties that seemed more promising. Denial of membership also would be a serious setback to the credibility of Western leaders, who formally pledged NATO enlargement in a 1994 NATO ministerial communiqué.

The Time for Decision

In sum, the allies must decide soon whether to persist in temporizing appeasement in the hope of taming the former Soviets or to pursue with temperate diplomatic reassurance to the Russians the course leading to expansion of the alliance. Nothing in the process of enlargement need rule out the possibility of erecting a security structure involving the Russians in tandem with NATO or of inviting further cooperation in other spheres between the former Soviet states and NATO. Indeed, it would seem desirable to couple any adjustments in NATO's role, as in the case of its recent involvement in ex-Yugoslavia, with opportunities for Russian engagement alongside the NATO allies.

For the United States, the course of enlargement is clearly preferable to further temporizing. Europe continues to need the reassurance of the American security guarantee, especially after the humiliating setbacks in the former Yugoslavia. Indeed, for the Europeans today, the question is not whether the Americans are needed but how best to consolidate the American vocation in Europe for the foreseeable future. This attitude is clearly reflected in the recent French posture toward NATO, which will likely lead shortly to full reintegration, accompanied by at least tacit acceptance by France for the first time since the Second World War of the inevitability of a major U.S. presence in Europe as an earnest of American engagement in the common pursuit of security. It is a new watershed in transatlantic affairs and should encourage Americans to understand that the commitment of the Western Europeans to partnership is now unequivocal. This, in turn, should help to broaden American understanding that it need not act alone in international undertakings and that it is to the advantage of the United States to cooperate with its allies across the spectrum of engagements in every sphere where conflicts arise, including security, trade, and finance.

Thus, the strengthening of NATO will lead to a strengthening of America's capacity for action in concert, with the multiplier effect that it offers the United States. Enlarging NATO will reinforce stability in the heart of Europe through new institutional links to the West. NATO expansion also will help to propel Europe in the direction of further consolidation within an expanding European Union, for NATO membership for Central and Eastern European states will reinforce the credentials of these applicants for EU membership. A stronger and broader EU will provide for the United States an even more reliable and responsible partnership with its European allies, whose shared values and goals will in turn reinforce the girders of mutual security at a time of profound change around the globe.

The United States and the Eurocorps

STEPHEN F. SZABO

Associate dean for academic affairs, Paul H. Nitze School of Advanced International Studies, Johns Hopkins University

The United States became a European power in the twentieth century, despite strong historical and domestic political traditions, for a number of reasons. The key reason behind what became a continuous involvement in European security after Pearl Harbor in 1941 was an interest in avoiding the dominance of Europe by one power, whether that power was Germany or the Soviet Union. A second reason was one restated in March 1996 by the secretary of state in Prague when Warren Christopher told his Czech audience that "we have an interest in your security, because we wish to avoid the instability that drew over 5 million Americans to fight in two world wars in Europe." This instability has been the result of nationalist rivalries and the inability of the European states to create a stable international order.

Europe after the fall of the Berlin Wall, the unification of Germany, and the collapse of the Soviet Union no longer faces the hegemonic threat of the Soviet Union. While this is a great and qualitative change for the better, it means that there is no longer a threat that unifies the United States and Europe. As Christoph Bertram has observed, threats are now divisive rather than unifying, coalition breaking rather than coalition forming. The threats that have surfaced tend to be like those of ethnic nationalism as found in the Balkans or the former Soviet Union, or even genocide or those associated with demographic change, modernization, and poverty as characterize the southern rim of the Mediterranean. These threats are often of an intrastate rather than interstate nature and are removed from the vital interests of the key states of the Continent. This new threat environment means that the need for collective defense as provided by the North Atlantic Treaty Organization (NATO) is declining rapidly and being replaced by the requirements of crisis management and the extension of a stable regime to these unstable areas.

Lessons for the United States

What consequences should the United States draw from these developments concerning its future role in European security? The first lesson to be learned has already been demonstrated in Bosnia, namely, that the United States will be a less reliable and predictable player in Europe than it was during the cold war. Its security interests will be less obvious in Bosnia or Moldova, for example, than they were in divided Berlin. The second lesson is that the end of the cold war does not mean the end of an American interest in a stable Europe nor does it mean that Americans can leave Europe to the Europeans. The specter of instability and a return to European nationalism remains, both in the Balkans and Eastern Europe but even within the larger democratic nations that are now experiencing the social and political tensions that accompany slow growth, demographic stagnation, and rising unemployment. Europe still lacks European leadership. There is no one to be held accountable to deal with new threats. There is still no 911 telephone number to be dialed in an emergency and from which a credible response can be expected.

While the United States will have to remain a European power, however, there is little reason for it to continue to play the same role it did during the cold war. In addition to the less direct threat posed to its interests by the local forest fires along Europe's periphery, pressing problems are being faced both at home and in Asia. Pressures for shifting attention to domestic problems will continue as defense budgets and, therefore, military capability decline. Asia, as well, will be demanding more of America's strategic attention over the next decade. Because Europe has developed a remarkable network of institutions and interlocking networks, it needs less American attention while the same cannot be said of Asia, where balance-of-power politics and the rise of a new potential hegemon require a large and continuing American presence.

A New Relationship

All these factors are leading to a looser and more flexible European-American security relationship in which the American role will become less central and in which the Europeans will have to carry a larger share of the burden. The formation of the Eurocorps is one means available to begin this unavoidable shift in the relationship. Other such initiatives include the newly formed European Force (EUROFOR) made up of 10,000 to 15,000 troops from Spain, Portugal, France, and Italy and a European Maritime Force (EUROMARFOR) of air and naval forces focused on the Mediterranean.

Formed by a Franco-German initiative in 1992, the Eurocorps was set up as a means of strengthening European security cooperation. The force, which became operational in November 1995, consists of 50,000 troops from Germany, France, Belgium, Luxembourg, and Spain. It may be an embryo of a future European military force that will be deployed under the auspices of either NATO or the Western European Union (although currently it is not formally a part of the Western European Union, WEU). The return of France to the military committee of NATO means that for the medium term at least the Eurocorps will develop within NATO rather than separately from it.

Many limits and contradictions surround the Eurocorps, including a continuing divergence between French desires to see it manage crisis reaction peacemaking missions outside of the traditional NATO area and a continuing German desire to use the force for primarily territorial defense missions in NATO Europe. The force, which consists largely of a French armored division and German mechanized brigades, is like all other European military forces in that it remains dependent on American capabilities in lift, reconnaissance, air cover, intelligence, and command and control. Its future has become more problematic in the wake of the French decision to professionalize and downsize its forces, including the elimination of the First Armored Division, which is the nucleus of the French contribution to the corps.

While the Eurocorps was initially opposed by the Bush administration, which feared it might become a rival to NATO, the Clinton administration has been more open to a European defense identity, and future American administrations should support it and other manifestations of a European willingness to develop military forces. Although American concerns about the possible unraveling of military integration are understandable, the United States will be able to sustain a continuing military role in Europe only if the Europeans demonstrate both a willingness and a capability to do more. Furthermore, earlier doubts that the Eurocorps might be separate from

NATO have been resolved. In addition, such multinational groupings are probably the best way to ensure that a credible European defense capability is maintained in an era of rising armaments costs and shrinking defense budgets. Contrary to the deeply held conviction of General Charles de Gaulle that public support for defense must rest on a national foundation, European defense may be sustainable in the future only on a multinational basis.

As the noncollective defense contingencies grow, the United States will have to find ways to allow the Europeans to use NATO assets to support missions undertaken by European forces. In other words, the United States should facilitate the formation of coalitions of those willing to deal with crises that do not justify a substantial American commitment of its own forces. It has already begun to move in this direction by the creation in NATO of Combined Joint Task Forces (CJTF), which are NATO task forces undertaken by those alliance members that wish to participate in a given military operation. These task forces will use NATO (that is, American capabilities) for the C3I, lift, and other functions that the Europeans do not possess to support largely European ground forces. Overall command of ground operations will be with a European NATO commander who could also be dual hatted as a WEU commander.

Implementation Force (IFOR) may be the test case for this concept after its initial mandate expires in December 1996. An IFOR II could become a NATO CJTF operated under a NATO command structure but with a scaled-down number of American ground forces. Lift, reconnaissance, intelligence, and command and control would continue to rely heavily on American capabilities, but the burden would shift more toward European ground forces. This shift would allow NATO to maintain a force to support civilian efforts in stabilizing the political settlement reached in Dayton but also permit the administration to honor its pledge to the American public to reduce the American military role in Bosnia without undermining a still fragile settlement.

In the future, the Eurocorps and other similar forces could be the structure for this new type of transatlantic security cooperation, allowing the United States to remain involved in a manner compatible with both its domestic environment and that of the new Europe.

The United States and a Common Foreign and Security Policy

W. Bruce Weinrod

Former U.S. deputy assistant secretary of defense

It is still too early to assess accurately the impact of Europe's Common Foreign and Security Policy through the European Union on U.S. foreign policy. What can be said is that any effects are likely to depend upon several key factors, including the nature of CFSP decision-making mechanisms, the relationship of CFSP to the North Atlantic Treaty Organization, and the width, depth, and nature of the overall EU institutional arrangements.

The first question that arises is, What would a CFSP mean operationally? The mechanisms by which decisions are made and implemented will have a practical effect on how a CFSP might affect foreign policy.

For routine diplomatic issues, a lengthy CFSP decision-making process, or complex implementation procedures, may simply mean irritating but nonetheless inconsequential delays in achieving U.S. objectives.

If, conversely, the particular foreign policy or security issue is important to the United States or requires rapid decision and implementation for its effectiveness, CFSP delays and complications could mean the difference between success and failure.

Suppose, for example, a security problem analogous to the Iraqi invasion of Kuwait. A real test for a CFSP in terms of U.S. interests is to ask what impact a CFSP might have on the likelihood of a common, concerted, rapid, and effective response by European nations, in cooperation with the United States, in a similar situation.

CFSP Decision-making Mechanisms

At least a part of the answer depends on the specific decision-making and implementing mechanisms of a European CFSP. It is theoretically possible for CFSP institutional mechanisms to be structured in ways that ensure that, if the requisite political will exists, the Europeans can cooperate with the United States.

A unanimous CFSP requirement would not affect U.S. interests if all the European nations were in support of an important U.S. foreign policy or security policy objective. In this situation, the existence of a CFSP could arguably contribute to the implementation of a rapid and cohesive response.

It is fair to say, however, that any CFSP that requires unanimity for decision making is likely at times to frustrate American foreign policy and security interests. Even in the Persian Gulf situation, for example, not all European nations were willing and ready to move as quickly and as intensively as was required.

CFSP mechanisms allowing for quick reaction would provide no assurance that response will occur. Nonetheless, the minimum necessary requirement would seem to be a CFSP procedural mechanism that allows European nations with significant military capabilities to take expeditious decisions and actions, even if others may be unwilling to act. This would at least make it less likely that a CFSP could frustrate a common U.S.-European response to serious foreign policy or security challenges.

CFSP and NATO

As a practical matter, however, one of the most important questions is how a CFSP would address its relationship to the North Atlantic Treaty Organization. To the surprise of many, and the chagrin of some, NATO has not only survived the end of the cold war but remains an essential ingredient for European security. Even France has decided that it must get closer to NATO.

The nature of a CFSP relationship to NATO will depend on the resolution of such issues as the scope, role, and capabilities of the Western European Union and the relationship of the WEU to NATO and the European Union.

Two important subplots will involve how Germany balances its strong interest in a smooth relationship with France with its arguably even stronger interest in a positive relationship with the United States and also how the French ultimately approach their military role in NATO.

NATO remains the primary framework for U.S. involvement in European and transatlantic security issues. From a U.S. perspective, it is essential that NATO, especially its military capabilities and effectiveness, not be damaged or undermined as a result of the establishment or implementation of a CFSP.

This requirement means at least two basic things: first, decisions and actions affecting transatlantic security would be made ultimately at NATO, and, second, any European military assets or capabilities could be established only in such a way that the result did not unnecessarily duplicate or divert resources away from NATO.

A separate but important issue for the United States will be the role in CFSP arrangements of several nations important to the United States. How, for example, would the nations of Central Europe be treated, and what would be Turkey's relationship to the CFSP? The U.S. interest should be in bringing these nations into any larger European decision-making mechanisms in ways that reinforce their integration into the Western democratic community of nations.

U.S. interests are clearly at stake in the outcome of a CFSP. The appropriate U.S. approach is simply to make clear the continuing essential importance of transatlantic foreign policy and security cohesion. A Europe seeking to go it alone or to develop and maintain military capabilities separate from, and equivalent to, those of NATO would be wasteful and counterproductive from a U.S. perspective.

The U.S. Focus

Thus, the United States should focus on the necessity of maintaining NATO's military assets and capabilities in an effective form and on assuring strong bilateral security ties as well with key European nations. As a practical matter, this attitude would require an open and positive relationship between the EU (and any military structures that may be placed under the EU) and NATO.

When common interests are challenged, however, the ultimate deciding factor will be political will. If the Europeans wish to respond to a foreign policy or security threat that the United States deems important, then the institutional arrangements of a CFSP can make this either easier or more difficult. But if the Europeans choose not to respond or wish to develop alternative approaches, then even the smoothest CFSP institutional arrangements are no guarantee that U.S. and European foreign policy and security relations will be harmonious.

What Kind of Europe?

This raises a final imponderable: will the development of an institutionalized CFSP, in and of itself, or in combination with other European trends, result in a Europe that believes that, even on the most central international issues, it must as a matter of course have policies separate, and perhaps even developed and implemented independently, from those of the United States? Or can a new Europe find it sensible to harmonize its policies on key international issues with those of the United States?

In the broadest sense, several geopolitical approaches are competing at present for Europe's future. There is the vision of a centralized Europe and the concept of a decentralized Europe (for each of these, there are the alternatives of a narrower or wider Europe). Finally, there is the vision of Europe as part of a larger transatlantic democratic community.

Europeans will have to sort these possibilities out for themselves. But, ultimately, the answers to these questions, much more than specific institutional arrangements, will determine the impact of a CFSP on U.S. interests.

The decision of the December 1996 EU summit, under the pressure of the Helms-Burton legislation to pressure publicly Cuba to move toward pluralist democracy and the observance of human rights, and also to threaten Cuba with a suspension of any trade agreements that may be reached in the future, is an encouraging development. Assuming this decision is implemented in practice, it could provide an example of how a CFSP and U.S. interests could in fact work smoothly together.

The challenge for statesmen on both sides of the Atlantic will be to ensure that the practical and institutional implementation of any new European arrangements is accomplished in such a way as to ensure that Europeans and Americans together can continue to protect and defend against any threats to their shared democratic values and institutions.

Crime and Cooperation: An American View

Jonathan Winer

U.S. deputy assistant secretary of state for law enforcement and crime

The law of unintended consequences has struck again. The collapse of ideological and economic barriers has not only opened the way for new political and economic expression; it has also unleashed international criminal syndicates eager to exploit the more open global environment that has followed the cold war. Today's international criminal organizations are as sophisticated and technologically literate as any legitimate multinational corporation. Often, they have many more resources to draw on, and they move freely between continents—sometimes more easily than legitimate corporations do.

Criminal organizations have perfected money-laundering techniques enabling them to accumulate obscene wealth while eluding many of the most sophisticated controls developed by the world's major industrial countries. But high-tech crime networks are not limited to laundering money. International car thieves use sealed containers to move their cars; alien and drug smugglers communicate through encrypted fax machines, cellular phones by satellite, and on the worldwide web; drug cartels use satellites to spot and report operations against their trade; and financial fraudsters not only rely on computers but maintain Internet addresses and even employ professional hackers to help them commit electronic information burglaries. In Colombia, the Cali cartel arranged with the Colombian phone company to permit it to eavesdrop systematically on law enforcement officials. Documents discovered in a raid on the offices of cartel chief Gilberto Rodriguez Orejuela showed that the kingpin had bought dozens of telephone company officials and had direct access to any telephone line he cared to listen to.

The threat that organized crime poses to governments is quickly emerging from the shadows to be ubiquitous and increasingly visible. We need not look far to see how pervasive the impact of organized crime can be. Every U.S. citizen pays higher insurance rates due to the number of cars stolen and transported abroad by international thieves. Every major U.S. city experiences crime that is the direct consequence of the emergence of ethnic-based gangs whose members include those illegally smuggled into the United States through the services of professional alien smugglers. And every community has in its midst cocaine and heroin produced thousands of miles from our shores, smuggled in by organized crime, and distributed by local criminals with ties to those overseas.

The Problem of Sovereignty

These criminals stop at no borders, but law enforcement officials must. In many aspects, traditional views of national sovereignty are now an obstacle to our efforts against transnational criminal activity, which violate every nation's sovereignty daily. Nations, for understandable reasons, find it extremely difficult to entrust other states with their information, laws, evidence, and even citizens. Many countries will not extradite their nationals to face criminal charges in other nations. Yet each nation is responsible, legally and politically, to its citizens—for protecting them against crime and for bringing criminals to justice. How is any nation to do so when a criminal can commit a crime in one jurisdiction and move to another to avoid detection and prosecution?

Thus, the dual nature of the modern global economy creates a real dilemma for governments. The director of enforcement for the U.S. Securities and Exchange Commission recently framed the issue in connection with financial crime:

> The tension that exists is how to facilitate a global market place and a global atmosphere in which capital can move between and among borders relatively freely and yet have in place standards and law enforcement intelligence mechanisms that do not permit or facilitate the laundering or the sanitizing of proceeds of organized crime or other criminal behavior.

Europe faced this issue in early 1996, as the governments of France and the Netherlands traded accusations concerning their own national drug policies, and France deferred moving forward with full implementation of the Schengen Agreement. Under Schengen, France and its close neighbors agreed to allow inside their borders, without independent checks, anyone who had been admitted to any other country in the region, which stretches through the heart of the original six-state European community and was due to extend further in the months to come. The French public had become increasingly anxious about the consequences of Schengen. Suppose another Schengen country let in a drug trafficker, terrorist, or other criminal? With Schengen in place, France perceived that it would have surrendered its ability to protect itself. While the French-Dutch squabble was ostensibly about the harmonization of European narcotics policy, French public fears about the impact of implementing the Schengen policy of no internal borders within Europe clearly fueled tensions.

Building Networks

The obvious answer, and one that governments have only just begun to act on, is to build networks for governments as capable and swift as the networks criminals use. If criminals can cross borders with ease to conduct their illegal business, governments must do the same. Nations must find new ways to get past old ideas about how sovereignty operates. After all, if only governments acknowledge sovereignty but criminals do not, sovereignty is already profoundly diminished.

The United States has been working aggressively to respond to the transnational crime problem and create such networks, especially with the Europeans. We have done this through a series of mutual legal assistance treaties, extradition treaties, and other arrangements designed to link governments together and ensure justice prevails regardless of the location of a criminal or a criminal act.

Despite these efforts, President Clinton recognized early in his administration that still more needed to be done. He commissioned a presidential review directive to determine what else the United States could do to deal with the internationalization of crime.

On October 22, 1995, President Clinton delivered a major foreign policy address at the fiftieth anniversary of the United Nations to more than 130 heads of state, calling for a global fight against transnational crime, terrorism, and drug trafficking. The president warned that "these forces (of international crime) jeopardize the global trend toward peace and freedom, undermine fragile democracies, sap the strength from developing countries, and threaten our efforts to build a safer, more prosperous world."

In conjunction with the speech, President Clinton issued the first presidential decision directive on international crime. This PDD declared that international criminal enterprises are not only a law enforcement problem but constitute a national security threat to the

United States. Under the PDD, President Clinton ordered that U.S. agencies produce greater results against this threat and authorized both unilateral and multilateral initiatives by the United States to combat crime.

These presidential actions had an immediate impact on U.S. allies. In the months that followed, serious discussions about additional actions against transnational crime took place with the European Union. Through the Transatlantic Dialogue, the EU and the United States signed a communiqué in Madrid in December 1995, specifying additional steps for new U.S.-EU cooperation against crime, including EU participation in the International Law Enforcement Academy in Budapest. Soon thereafter, the United States agreed to negotiate a new agreement on cooperation against the trade in precursor chemicals used in making cocaine and other illicit drugs. This agreement should be concluded by the end of 1996. Senior law enforcement officials and diplomats joined together in the G-7 plus Russia to make new commitments to solving problems of mutual legal assistance and extradition, explicitly endorsing the concept of no safe haven. Within the G-7 came new commitments to ending the practice of state-sponsored commercial bribery, including the tax deductibility of bribes in some countries. The Organization for Economic Cooperation and Development in Europe also began moving on long-stalled antibribery standards. The EU joined the United States to focus new assistance to the Caribbean, a major drug transit zone, as a means of fighting drugs. The United States and Japan agreed in their common agenda to find ways to cooperate more closely on law enforcement. And the United States, United Kingdom, France, and the Netherlands found new ways to cooperate in maritime operations to interdict drugs moving by sea in the Caribbean, long an area of divided jurisdictions and responsibilities.

This kind of cooperation has yet to create a full and complete transnational network for governments as flexible and effective as that needed to be ahead of the criminals. But the transnational network of governments against crime, like so many other new networks in this globalized world, is being built and is growing rapidly every day.

ABBREVIATIONS

ASEAN	Association of South East Asian Nations
BDI	Federation of German Industry
CAP	Common Agricultural Policy
CEFTA	Central European Free Trade Area
CET	Common External Tariff
CFSP	Common Foreign and Security Policy
CJTF	Combined Joint Task Forces
CSCE	Conference on Security and Cooperation in Europe
EBRD	European Bank for Reconstruction and Development
EC	European Community
ECB	European Central Bank
EDC	European Defense Community
EEC	European Economic Community
EFTA	European Free Trade Association
EMS	European Monetary System
EMU	European Monetary Union
EPC	European Political Cooperation
ERM	Exchange Rate Mechanism
ECSC	European Coal and Steel Community
EU	European Union
EURATOM	European Atomic Energy Community
EUROFOR	European Force
EUROMARFOR	European Maritime Force

GATT	General Agreement on Tariffs and Trade
IFOR	Implementation Force
IGC	Intergovernmental Conference
NACC	North Atlantic Cooperation Council
NAFTA	North American Free Trade Agreement
NATO	North Atlantic Treaty Organization
OECD	Organization for Economic Cooperation and Development
OEEC	Organization for European Economic Cooperation
OSCE	Organization for Security and Cooperation in Europe
PFP	Partnership for Peace
SEA	Single European Act
SFOR	Stabilization Force
TAFTA	Transatlantic Free Trade Area
UN	United Nations
UNPROFOR	United Nations Protection Force
WEU	Western European Union
WTO	World Trade Organization

CHRONOLOGY OF THE EUROPEAN UNION

MARCH 1947: The Truman Doctrine establishes American commitment to defend the cause of free peoples and to contain Soviet power. The Treaty of Dunkirk establishes a French-British alliance against a future German threat.

JUNE 1947: U.S. Secretary of State George Marshall offers aid for the reconstruction of Europe (Marshall Plan).

MARCH 17, 1948: The Brussels Treaty establishes an alliance between France, Britain, and the Benelux states for collective defense against the Soviet Union.

APRIL 1948: The Organization for European Economic Cooperation (OEEC) is established to administer the Marshall Plan.

MAY 1948: The Congress of Europe is held at The Hague.

APRIL 1949: The North Atlantic Treaty Organization (NATO) is established.

MAY 1949: The Council of Europe is created.

JUNE 1950: A European Defense Community (EDC) is proposed.

APRIL 18, 1951: The Treaty of Paris, which established the European Coal and Steel Community (ECSC) is signed.

AUGUST 1954: France rejects the EDC, and the EDC fails.

OCTOBER 1954: The Western European Union (WEU) is created.

JUNE 2, 1955: ECSC-member foreign ministers, meeting in Messina, decide to extend integration to all economic sectors.

MARCH 25, 1957: The Treaty of Rome, establishing the European Economic Community (EEC) and the European Atomic Energy Community (Euratom), is signed.

JANUARY 1, 1958: The Treaty of Rome enters into force.

JANUARY 1960: The Stockholm Convention establishes the European Free Trade Association (EFTA).

DECEMBER 14, 1960: The OEEC becomes the Organization for Economic Cooperation and Development (OECD), with the addition of Canada and the United States.

JULY 1962: The Common Agricultural Policy (CAP) is introduced.

APRIL 1965: The Fusion Treaty forms a single European Commission, merging the ECSC, EEC, and Euratom.

JULY 1965: France boycotts EC institutions.

JANUARY 1966: France resumes its position in the Council of Europe.

JULY 1967: The Fusion Treaty enters into force.

JULY 1, 1968: The customs union introducing the Common External Tariff (CET) is completed.

DECEMBER 1969: The Hague summit opens discussion of enlargement, monetary union, and adoption of a plan to implement the CAP.

JUNE 1970: Negotiations on EC membership begin with Denmark, Ireland, Norway, and the United Kingdom.

SEPTEMBER 1972: Norway withdraws its proposed membership after a referendum.

JANUARY 1, 1973: Denmark, Ireland, and the UK join the European community.

DECEMBER 1974: EC leaders agree on direct elections to the European Parliament.

MARCH 1975: The first meeting of the European Council is held in Dublin.

JULY 1978: France and Germany propose a European Monetary System (EMS).

MARCH 1979: The EMS enters into force.

JUNE 1979: The first direct elections to the European Parliament are held.

JANUARY 1, 1981: Greece joins the European Community.

FEBRUARY 1984: A European Parliament Draft Treaty establishes the European Union.

JUNE 1984: The Western European Union is reactivated.

DECEMBER 1985: The European Council proposes a Single European Act (SEA) for economic revival and a common market.

JANUARY 1, 1986: Portugal and Spain join the European Community.

FEBRUARY 1986: The Single European Act is signed.

FEBRUARY 1987: The European Commission adopts a plan of action for implementation of the Single European Act.

JULY 1987: The Single European Act enters into force.

MARCH 27, 1990: Portugal and Spain enter the Western European Union.

OCTOBER 3, 1990: German unification is complete.

DECEMBER 1990: Intergovernmental Conferences on Economic and Monetary Union and on Political Union open.

APRIL 5, 1991: The European Bank for Reconstruction and Development (EBRD) is founded.

FEBRUARY 7, 1992: The Treaty on European Union (EU) is signed in Maastricht.

JANUARY 1, 1993: Introduction of the single European Market and the European Economic Area.

NOVEMBER 1, 1993: The Maastricht Treaty enters into force.

JANUARY 1, 1995: Austria, Finland, and Sweden join the EU.

1999: The introduction of a single European Currency is anticipated.

Sources:
Europa, the home page of the European Union, http://europa.eu.int/en/eu/hist/euchron.html.

William Nicoll and Trevor C. Salmon, *Understanding the New European Community* (New York: Harvester Wheatsheaf, 1990).

A NOTE ON THE BOOK

This book was edited by Ann Petty,
Dana Lane, and Cheryl Weissman
of the Publications Staff
of the American Enterprise Institute.
The text was set in Palatino,
a typeface designed by
the twentieth-century Swiss designer Herman Zapf.
Cynthia Stock,
of Silver Spring, Maryland, set the type,
and Edwards Brothers Incorporated,
of Lillington, North Carolina,
printed and bound the book,
using permanent acid-free paper.

The AEI Press is the publisher for the American Enterprise Institute for Public Policy Research, 1150 Seventeenth Street, N.W., Washington, D.C., 20036; *Christopher C. DeMuth,* publisher; *Dana Lane,* director; *Ann Petty,* editor; *Leigh Tripoli,* editor; *Cheryl Weissman,* editor; *Jennifer Lesiak,* editorial assistant.